PEARSON   ALWAYS LEARNING

Debra Stevens

Making Sense
A Guide to Sound Reasoning and Critical Thinking

Eighth Edition

Cover Art: Courtesy of Photodisc/Getty Images.

Pearson Learning Solutions, 330 Hudson Street, New York, New York 10013
A Pearson Education Company
www.pearsoned.com

Printed in the United States of America

000200010271971984

TG/KE

ISBN 10: 1-323-31106-8
ISBN 13: 978-1-323-31106-6

19 2022

Copyright Acknowledgments

Contents

Preface

First let me explain the purpose of this book: to help the readers think and communicate better. Now let me explain what the purpose is not. The purpose of this book is not to instruct in formal logic or rhetoric/persuasion, although there is some of that in the chapters. The emphasis throughout is on conscious thinking about language and control of our speech, especially when responding to others in an attempt to facilitate clearer, more responsible discussions. This requires careful listening and discernment. The language analysis tools are key to developing this discernment. The book also is designed to be useful as critical thinking course material, since it contains lessons and exercises for instructors and students. Of course, it could be used by anyone trying to improve his/her critical thinking skills.

The most important lesson in this entire book is the first, "Observation." Here readers develop an ability that they already have to some degree, the ability to *observe carefully* and question what they believe they *see*. The next step is to observe and question language. Readers describe what they see and hear with objective language. They become aware of different rhetorical methods that can be used to slant facts.

Chapter Two, "Distinguishing Fact from Opinion," helps students question first impressions. It makes them practice suspending judgments. It analyzes language closely to help students question statements that may sound factual but are in reality just opinion. Practice exercises allow readers to test their skills in writing concretely and factually. As well, this chapter includes a clear explanation of "facts" and "evidence," i.e., what constitutes a fact and what qualifies as evidence. It also gives the reader a critical lesson to develop an appreciation for the need to qualify studies as well as "experts and authorities" if they are to be relied upon for research support.

Chapter Three explains "premises" and teaches how to identify them in speech and writing. It also instructs in how to use them in one's own reasoning processes. The section on discerning, reading, or listening for premises teaches readers how to focus on key words. They learn to question a premise when it is evident and to ask for one when it is not readily apparent in the other person's speech or writing. Supplementary reading material at the end of the book should be used, as should outside sources, so that students can practice this skill. They should read and ask themselves, "What must the writer believe in order to make this assertion?" instead of assuming they know the values of the writer.

While reading Chapter Four, Definition, readers may take time to think and learn about language; they learn to *use definition to clarify issues*. The definition section causes readers to think before they speak. It also teaches them to *question other people's words as opposed to attacking their persons*. Lessons on using figurative language are also given for those who want to speak more imaginatively while still staying objective. This section is useful for analyzing everything from political speeches to a family member's sometimes round-about ways of saying things. It is also a must for anyone trying to avoid being misinterpreted when speaking before groups. This is a lengthy chapter, but it gets students to really think about language and how important language mastery is to the reasoning process.

Once readers can analyze language and discern premises, Chapter Five, "Causal Reasoning," will make them question their methods of reasoning about causes. This section teaches students to think logically before assigning a specific cause to a specific effect. This entails some lessons in more formal logic, but it does not require any knowledge of this subject per se. This section merely stops people from making illogical misconnections between cause and effect, those kinds of hasty connections heard in the media after the Columbine High School incident, or more recently, in reference to reasons for war.

Please note: This is not a book on how to win arguments. We do not need to know how to make points and appear to be right. We need to learn how to think and speak honestly, with integrity. Developing integrity in one's thinking begins with carefully observing and questioning what one believes one sees and hears. This is how we start out on the road to reasoning. Thus, Chapter Six, "Logical Fallacies," creates a clear set of rules for avoiding faulty reasoning, rules that will make sense by the time the reader has reached this chapter. Here are listed definitions and examples of logical fallacies that should be avoided if one wants to write or speak reasonably. Also included is a practice test.

Chapter Seven, titled "Readings," contains some further readings to allow the critical thinker to apply his/her skills. Here there are two articles, one by psychologist Carl Rogers on communication that is quite interesting to most students; a Socratic dialogue that includes "The Allegory of the Cave"; the Declaration of Independence, which is very useful for practicing premises; and a short work of fiction that allows students to practice ethical reasoning. Thus, students have a variety of genres with which to practice their critical analysis skills. We learn another valuable lesson: Critical thinking can make a variety of reading experiences more fulfilling and enlightening. The reader can apply the skills to understand the author's point of view and reasoning and to examine their own thinking habits. "Despicable Us" by Frank Bruni enlightens us as to ways journalists shape news. Maggie Jackson's "Distracted" enlightens us regarding ways tech can alter our perceptions, values and behavior.

There are also three appendices with recommended supplemental texts and videos, exercises, instructions for how to cite texts, and a glossary of terms. Instructors of critical thinking should probably access these appendices before planning the syllabus and conducting research.

I hope you will find this book interesting and enjoyable. Have fun testing your understanding by doing the exercises in each section. Start with the pretest to see how much critical thinking you already use. Test your friends (not your boss) and see how well they do. Whatever you do, don't be too hard on yourself. Much of this is new. Also give yourself credit for one thing right now: You're on the right road. You're reading this book! I hope critical thinking skills allow you to start **making** some **sense** out of the world around you.

Pretest

Answer TRUE or FALSE (Answers on next page)

1. _____ The following is a fact: "Body language informs you what a person is feeling or thinking."

2. _____ Statistics are facts.

3. _____ The goal of a critical thinker is to prove he/she is right.

4. _____ This is an objective statement: "The woman was aggressive and vicious, so she was obviously on drugs."

5. _____ Latin people display affection more openly than the British.

6. _____ One way to help prevent miscommunications is to question other people's reasoning.

7. _____ There is always more than one cause to an effect.

8. _____ This is a fact: "Studies show that low-income children from broken homes have trouble related to drug and alcohol abuse."

9. _____ This is an exaggeration: "We all know that seniors are treacherous on the roadways, causing high incidences of accidents."

10. _____ Suspending judgments while listening to another person's explanation is necessary if one is to maintain good, clear communication.

11. _____ Violent video games cause kids to act violently.

12. _____ Women are more emotional than men.

13. _____ The term "sexual harassment" has objective and subjective meaning.

14. _____ "Going under anesthesia? Sure, it's risky, but so is walking across the street." This is a good, sound analogy (comparison of a situation or condition).

15. _____ Your boss is trying to make you miserable.

Answers to Pretest

1. False Body language may suggest, but it does not inform you.

2. False Factual information may come from statistics. Not always.

3. False Read the first chapter of this book.

4. False "Vicious" and "aggressive" are subjective words (opinions).

5. False This is hyperbole and is also subjectively worded.

6. True Questioning another's reasoning can clarify the discussion.

7. True Right. Can you think of anything that has only one cause?

8. False Again, the language here is not factual. Also, which studies? It is an assertion of a fact (studies were done is implied) and an interpretation (have shown) with no basis.

9. True It is an exaggeration. "We all know" and "seniors" implies all seniors are "treacherous."

10. True Forming judgments before the discussion has ended probably means you are not listening while you are judging.

11. False No "one cause," and the language is abstract, subjective.

12. False Just what does "emotional" mean and how does one gauge it?

13. True There is both a legal (objective) and personal (subjective) definition.

14. False The two situations are too dissimilar.

15. Either (Does your boss really have to *try*?)

CHAPTER ONE

Observation

Look Before Leaping

A critical thinker looks before leaping. Observation, seeing only what is present, questioning what you think you see, and noticing what is not there, is the first step to critical thinking. We will start out on this long road to critical thinking by repeatedly practicing observing things and people. We will then move on to observing language. Be aware at the outset: Effort on the part of your brain is required. This process may be hazardous to blissful ignorance. When you are asked to observe, you are asked to see and hear and focus on one subject over a period of time and while doing so avoid making assumptions. Keep in mind the reward—knowledge. Reasoning via observing objectively isn't easy, but once you are through the process, you will feel more confident in your assessments and judgments.

I've taught critical thinking for twenty-five years at the city college level. The first day of class, we discuss what it means to observe. We question what we think we "know" from observing people, animals, and television. Most of my students aren't scientists, mechanics, or engineers, professionals used to practicing careful observation. They also don't intend to major in science or engineering. They don't see any need to practice "seeing." They think they "know" what they "see." I show them Escher prints. They look at ads on television or in *Rolling Stone* or the *New Republic*. They practice observing photographs or drawings. They practice analyzing and evaluating the claims made next to the pictures. Let's carefully observe and consider a graphic in order to illustrate the problem. First let me tell you where it came from and how I happened to see it. It's good practice to put pictures, and quoted words, in context.

So, here I am, in my home, on my couch, eating Wheaties. On the news, I *hear* an assertion concerning mass gravesites found in Kosovo. No one tells me who found them or where in Kosovo these graves are located. No *proof* is offered during this broadcast, except the picture, which is kept onscreen while people describe mass killings. All I *see* is something that purportedly is an aerial photograph of a mass gravesite. What I *know* is that people are putting this picture on my television screen and they are providing a context, a surrounding story. They talk over the images of "mass gravesites," which are held on the screen for about half a minute. Other pictures of dead bodies on a roadside periodically interrupt the gravesite image.

One picture of a mass gravesite looks something like this:

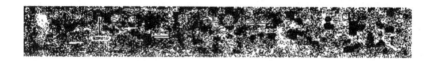

This may well have been a mass gravesite. That is not the *question at issue* here. From observing the picture, I could not say I was convinced it definitely was. If I were going to believe that there were mass gravesites in Kosovo as I watched this news coverage, I certainly was not going to be convinced by this picture. All I could say was that it could *possibly* represent a gravesite. It could possibly represent a missile site. Honestly, I couldn't testify that the picture I was seeing there was ground at all. They said it was a picture from the sky, a picture of the ground in Kosovo. Okay, I believed them. I took their word for that, but a gravesite? Maybe.

Am I just being a paranoid, Berkeley liberal? Is it wrong to question something so serious? No. I am questioning the evidence, which I should do in any case that is put forward for me to evaluate. I am a mom, a teacher, and a citizen. As a citizen, I am not going to believe a picture represents something just because Ms. Sassy on Channel 55 says it does. Sure, she has given me a context, a way to interpret, and a name for the picture (mass gravesite). Sure, I am inclined to believe her. But, I do have questions. As I said, I am a citizen. This same idea applies to other contexts. For example, I am not going to vote for people based only on what they say or on what they promise. I cannot really *observe* their values, their character, on television or YouTube. I can perceive only the persona they are projecting at the moment. So, what will I do about it? I will observe their records as state representatives and then assess their value as reasonable, knowledgeable, credible individuals. I *will* believe the records of how they have voted. I will not believe what they promise, although a tax cut and tuition credits sure sound good, don't they? (I WANT TO BELIEVE!)

Using **objective observation**, which means observing over a period of time to discern facts, understand reality, consider situations, things, people from different angles, we can get a clearer, more comprehensive picture from which to make our interpretations. What meaning does the gravesite picture have for you now? It represents your first attempt at applying the first step to **objective reasoning** using this text.

Barriers to Objective Observation

What you must be aware of from the outset is that "meaning" or value is assigned by *you*. The value you assign to something depends on your past, and thus depends on what is in your head at the moment. **Subjective** interpretations, personal habits of reading into the object to see what you expect to see, or what you want to see, are not useful. This is what we want to avoid.

Many kinds of barriers to observing exist. Some of the barriers are inherent in human nature. Some are self-imposed. For whatever reason, people can fool us, and we can fool them. Additionally, we bring biases to the table, and with these we may try to control other people's views. Anyone belonging to a family unit, functional or dysfunctional or somewhere in between, knows about barriers. Psychologists may call them defense mechanisms, but I don't like the machinelike association. I just call them barriers which prevent us from seeing clearly. They impair our ability to see the facts. Sometimes we don't want to see things objectively.

Take my son, for example. He wakes his sister up with his music. She complains that he woke her up. He replies, "It wasn't that loud." Is he being objective? No. He's being defensive and subjective. He is avoiding the question at issue, which is, "Did the music wake her up?" The answer is, "Why, yes, it did." This in turn means the music was loud enough to wake her up, which means he was rather inconsiderate. He should have lowered the music so as to not possibly awaken her.

If we want people to understand us, to get to "know" us, and communicate honestly with us, we must lower the barriers, sort of like what they did with the Berlin wall. Before we lower the wall, we must trust. That's what most people find difficult to do, which perhaps perpetuates many of the barriers beyond which we cannot or choose not to observe. The article by Carl Rogers in Chapter 7 of this book speaks eloquently regarding the effects of these barriers and gives us some solid motivation for withdrawing them in order to facilitate better, clearer communication.

Yet another problem people face when it comes to trying to observe one another is this: Sometimes, if not often in our everyday routines, we find it unnecessary to stop and look and question what we think we *see*. It's easier just to *assume* we know. We do this at home, at work, and on our mass transit excursions. We label and judge things we see or hear and put no more thought into the matter. We are content to believe that we know this person's "type," for example, as she meanders through the supermarket aisles with three energetic children in tow, then arrives at the checkout counter with her coupons. We judge her and blame her, although we don't know her. That keeps things simple. No strain. We put people in our mental boxes with labels on them and go about our mindless, daily business. So, what's wrong with that? Well, it is not fair, not thinking objectively. If we aren't thinking objectively, we aren't reasoning.

Here is an example to illustrate what happens when we don't question but rather simply label what we see, label things and people, purely out of habit. In the seventh book of his *Republic* (reprinted in Chapter 7 of this text), Plato gives us a dialogue between two speakers, Socrates and his student Glaucon. This dialogue consists of an allegory, a exemplary narrative that uses symbols to represent rather abstract concepts. The allegory, as told by Socrates, shows how men, chained up in a cave all their lives are unable to "see" past the cave and images, or "shadows," which are created via some firelight off to the side. These men are quite mistaken as to what they think is real. They believe the shadows, which play against the wall, shadows of men moving back and forth carrying objects, are real. They do not, cannot perceive any substance beyond their narrow scope of vision. Their necks and bodies are chained so that they can't look around, question, or compare. They can converse with one another, but, as you can imagine, their conversations are rather limited.

This is where the story gets interesting. Socrates says that if these men are brought out into the sunlight too fast, they will be in pain, perceiving the light of truth (reality) too quickly. He says they will adjust, though. It will take time to learn to objectively observe reality. They will see that individual things and people have depth and substance. The question then becomes, who will return to the cave and help those other guys out? (This whole story came to mind as I watched *The Matrix*.)

Reasonable, inquisitive people are not cave dwellers. They observe circum-spectly, from different angles, before they begin to assume what something is, before they try to label it. They use "circumspection," which means a circular vision. No, they don't spin their heads around like Regan in *The Exorcist*. That would be really painful. If someone observes circumspectly, he/she checks out all the angles.

Do the liberated cave dwellers read fine print in contracts? You bet they do. It may be painful, but they do. No paying 3.9 percent for three months and then 19.9 percent all the months after. If Mrs. Beezley calls me up and offers me some great deal for a nifty new cell phone, well, suffice it to say, she soon wishes she had skipped my number. I can't observe her over the phone. Observing her wouldn't be that helpful, anyway. (That too could be painful!) What do I need to observe? I need the contract, but I don't have it.

Well, this is where the definition of "observation" takes on an additional meaning for our purposes. In lieu of literally "seeing" the document, I need to see the information in her head, the truth about this splendid deal she is offering me. How do I do that? I question the picture of my happiness that she has offered me so far. I question the claims she makes, and question to find out what she isn't allowing me to see. She doesn't want me to see a picture of me, say, ten months from now opening my bill and throwing this nifty new phone out the window. So, what specific questions should I ask? What should I try to release from her storehouse of knowledge?

Getting the truth out of people, getting them to lower the barriers and open their minds enough so that we can actually converse with them, can take serious effort, but it is worth it in the long run if we want to avoid misunderstanding. First we have to get straight what we want: What is the *question at issue?*

If I am talking to the phone saleslady and she doesn't have the answers to my questions, what should I do? Well, I won't let her limit my vision of the contract she is proposing over the phone. I will keep asking questions. Such salespeople who stay with me usually inevitably end up offering to send the printed contract to me through the mail. I'm happy.

Go Ahead and Ask!

Let's talk for a minute about what causes people to not question other people who offer them shadowy pictures. One reason people elect to remain in the cave is that it might be considered rude to raise a question, lift their heads and look someone in the eye, express doubt about what they are supposed to see.

Let me ask such people this: Isn't it rude of people to call you up during your day and offer to sell you something you did not ask for? Isn't it rude for them to assume you have nothing better to do with your time? Isn't it rude for people to solicit you with what is usually misinformation, because it is only half or a quarter of the whole story? Finally, are you respecting yourself, allowing yourself to be run over like this? You, I would submit, are being rude to yourself. So, cut it out. Get out of the cave. The sun is shining out here. You may not get the whole truth, but you will be going in the right direction by asking for it. It's not being rude or nerdy. It's taking responsibility and thinking of yourself as smart. Believe me, it feels good to say to yourself, "Gee, that was smart of me!"

Have you learned anything about yourself so far as you have been reading and thinking things over? You should be able to see that your ability to control what you "see" is limited. Limited by what? Well, lots of things. What you have developed is a way of seeing. Why do you see things the way you do? That's a question you will have to try *making sense* out of.

Seeing as much of the whole picture as you can is essential. Think of any time you went to purchase a used car. What did you notice first?

Now answer this question: How important would that aspect of the vehicle be to your ultimate satisfaction with that car twelve months away?

Habits, habitual ways of seeing, limit us. **Conditioning**, a process by which we develop habitual responses to given stimuli, is relied upon by advertisers, photojournalists, caretakers, and even teachers. Conditioning is not necessarily bad, but when we are operating purely out of habit, we need to step back and question, just every once in a while, just why we are responding or behaving in a certain way?

Many of us have been conditioned to value a car for its overall appearance as opposed to its overall functioning capabilities. We say, "Hey, cool car." Some of you look under the car, to see if it's dry down there. Some of you even look under the hood. Some of you try the radio. Some of you check out the trunk. Most of you drive the car before buying it. What do you observe while driving? How much observing, seeing and hearing, and feeling/sensing do you get to do in your fifteen-minute test drive? Are you listening to the car's motor, the transmission or listening to the radio while the salesman is talking to you while you take your test drive? Try to notice things that are important and if the salesman is about to turn on that radio and jabber in your ear, ask him to please not do that so you can listen to the motor.

Listening to people is a little more difficult. You are in far less control, for various reasons. Those habits of not-listening you may have developed over time, known as tuning out and waiting for your turn to talk, can be unlearned. Once you admit you have a habit of doing this, you can work on it. To motivate you, consider this: you don't like it when you sense someone is doing this while you are speaking, do you? Remember how you felt the last time someone did this? Can you recall just how that discussion went? Was it a fruitful conversation or something else? Try objectively observing people closely as you are speaking to them some time. Note their eye contact, head or hand movements. You may achieve some enlightenment about others by doing this and if you are really objective, you will learn something about yourself.

Looking for Behavioral Meaning & Patterns: Oversimplifications

We have bad thinking habits when it comes to language interpretation. We have been lead to believe in people profiling, have been lead to think of ourselves as amateur psychologists. Believe me, no psychologist worth his degree would be so clumsy as to jump to a conclusion as to a person's attitude based on a minute's observation of his or her body language. Animals have predictable patterns. People are more complex. I keep telling my students:

You're not just animals

They don't accept my opinion. Oh well. Like I said, we will discuss this later, but for now, I would hope that no psychologists, and none of my students, would presume to "know" anything about a person's attitude based solely on a brief observation. What we all should do, if we want to get to know others, is observe and keep notes. Not actual physical notes on a pad. That would be silly and possibly dangerous. No, we should take mental notes, and if we have a theory and are considering something, some pattern of behavior as being "evidence," we should ask the person questions: "I noticed you scratch your head a lot. Do you have dandruff?" is not nice. Don't ask embarrassing or leading questions. However, if you think someone is sad based on his/her hunched over posture, ask, "Are you okay? You seem to be a bit hunched over." Don't assume anything.

Consider slowing down before jumping to conclusions, and even consider putting into words what you think you see if the conclusions you are trying to reach are important. Remember the distinctions we have made here between observing and interpreting.

Puppy Purchase: Observing vs. Interpreting

I once got it into my head that my kids needed a puppy. My daughter and I went to two places, a pound and a humane society. At the pound, the puppies were in cages. The "cute" puppy I saw, the one that I wanted badly to bundle up and throw into the back seat of my car to keep forever and ever (remember my kids needed a puppy), was small enough to meet our requirements. It was cute. Mary, my daughter, made that girl noise at it: "Oh, how cute." She tried to squish her fingers through the cage to pet it. The puppy licked her fingertips. It looked like a done deal. But, wait a minute, I said to myself. How could I know how this puppy would behave? I might put it in my car and it might urinate on the seat, first thing. It might chew my pseudo-leather car seats. I thought about it and remembered hearing that the humane society let people take the dogs out into a yard and actually "get to know" the animals. We went there next and took one puppy out into the yard. He appeared sweet while in the cage, even affectionate, slobbering all over our fingers, but once we got him out in the open, he just wanted to chase anything that moved. He didn't even look back at us in the whole time (twenty minutes) we sat there. My point here is that people are like this.

You need to take time to see people in action before you label them. You meet someone over the Internet, and it seems great. But then you meet him and go out with him and it's a different story. Not that he urinates all over your car or goes scampering around under trees, chasing leaves while you're out standing in line at the movies. The guy probably won't chew your furniture when you invite him into your home after a few dates, but I bet you will get a chance to see if he wipes his feet on the mat, or returns his glass to the sink, or helps you to set the table, and you will get a chance to hear if and how he burps and if he says "excuse me." Not that you can "know" anything for sure by observing these behaviors, but you can have a better chance of "getting to know" a person through repeated, careful observation. There's not much observing you can do just by reading someone's words. Writers manipulate language and manipulate facts to make things appear and sound both acceptable and pleasing to you. I know.

In any event, the final stage to observing is questioning what you have observed. What did you see? What did you not see? People traditionally do not show us their bad sides. But what if they do?

They Drive Me Crazy!: On the Road

Observing takes patience and time, but it pays off. Charles Darwin's gardener once told an interviewer that he really did not know what to make of him: "Poor man, he just stands and stares at yellow flowers for minutes at a time." You may not be working to perfect your understanding of nature, but there is one situation I think you can relate to.

Imagine you are driving down a road close to home. A car is tailgating you. Let's make the car one of those SUVs, you know, the 4x4's, the ones that rugged suburbanites use. Now, you have observed this behavior for about six blocks. You have tried glaring at the individual from your rearview mirror, which has had *no* visible effect. You have tried to slow down and speed up, but this has not been helpful. So, here you are, helpless, being tailgated by this SUV, this hulk used mostly to transport this "rugged individual," this "so-and-so" to non-rugged places. You clench your teeth and grip the wheel as you hear yourself hissing vile words. Your body becomes more tense and your neck is starting to hurt from all the bobble-head motion, i.e., looking in the rear view mirror, looking ahead just for a second, then scowling into the side mirror. Anyone watching your head movements would think either you've been hypnotized to think you're a chicken or you need an exorcist! You are desperately suppressing a desire to slam on your brakes. What can you do? Imagine a bigger picture. Broaden your perspective. Escape tunnel vision. You've locked yourself into a very small vista. Look around you. Look up ahead. The cars are going slower. Widen the lens. You can see brake lights. This person is in a hurry. Change into the right lane and let him pass. See him speed up and reach the red light before you do. Laugh, "Aha!" Your emotional distance, obtained from observing the whole picture, taking yourself out of the confines of your usual smaller, constricted perspective, has made a ridiculous situation "funny and ridiculous" instead of "ridiculous and dangerous." Now that's objective observation!

DISCUSSION 1.1

Try writing about a time wherein you found yourself either employing the first step to critical thinking, objective observation and analysis, or not. Explain enough so your reader can understand causes and effects, as one can from reading the two examples above. Just about 100 words, again, like the examples above.

How to Objectively Observe Language: *Listen!*

When listening, critical thinkers really listen and make every effort to suspend emotions. They strive to remain detached before they become affected by the speaker's words. They reject the tendency to have kneejerk reactions to even the most painful language. They learn to *separate the person from the person's words.*

Critical thinkers also have to separate their own reactions from what another person is actually saying. For starters, we will try to just admit, maybe we are not understanding what the person means. We might be wrong.

We also have to keep in mind what we are after in our communications with others. Our purpose in learning to listen objectively is neither to win arguments nor to master the gentle art of turning people's own words against them to make them look bad. We're not politicians or rhetoricians. The object of this lesson is to give you some help so that you can improve your ability to communicate and the first step to that is listening. When listening and looking for *reasonableness* in a text, we must consider the words as elements of communication and distinguish between decorative, emotional and informative language. First let's look at some of the more decorative language people with stylistic "flair" tend to use to entertain and perhaps catch people up so that they go along with their "apparent" reasoning.

Language Fluffery

Most reasonable people look for the significance of what is being said. We first look for import, information. Critical thinkers have to work harder than even most reasonable people, though. If we don't understand some words, we consider the *context* in which the words appear. We also try to demand objective language of ourselves when we write or speak. *What we don't consider* as meaningful is the "fluffy" kind of language that people can use to clutter up ideas.

In this book, we'll learn different types of emotional appeals and rhetorical manipulations. George Orwell, author of *1984* and *Animal Farm*, called this type of fluffy language (in his essay "Politics and the English Language") "meaningless words." Meaningless words are those that are overused, broad, euphemistic, or otherwise vague. Meaningless words can cause ambiguity and confusion.

I think people recognize logical language when they hear it, and they know the truth when they hear it, and sometimes become frustrated when they read or hear in the media what they know is just downright untrue. On the other hand, people somehow recognize a statement that has the "ring of truth" to it.

Parallelism

Although the rhetorical device known as parallelism sounds nice and is a good mnemonic device, it often sounds hollow when we observe what's behind it, question the meaning of the statement. For example, when OJ Simpson said "I would not. I could not. I did not kill my wife" (which one comedian noted sounded like something from Dr. Seuss), we might have thought "Hmm. Sounds good." It has rhythm and rhyme, a repetition of a grammatical pattern, but this *parallelism* does not really stand up as evidence of his innocence.

Parallelism is common in political speech:

> "Ask not what your country can do for you; ask what you can do for your country."
>
> —John F. Kennedy (Inaugural Address 1961)

It is nice and rhythmic, but we have to ask: What is it saying? What does it mean? Parallelism is taught in speech class. If you have taken a speech class you know the definition: it is a repetition of a grammatical pattern that is sonorous and easy to remember, a mnemonic device.

Parallelism sounds nice, and I am not suggesting you not use it or criticize others who include it in their writing or speech. Just don't let it obscure meaning. Ask questions if something is unclear. However, if you hear some language that both makes sense, has substance and is nice sounding, count yourself lucky and study such writers closely to learn how to write (or speak) that well:

> I have a dream that one day this nation will rise up and live out the true meaning of its creed: "We hold these truths to be self-evident: that all men are created equal." I have a dream that one day on the red hills of Georgia the sons of former slaves and the sons of former slave owners will be able to sit down together at a table of brotherhood. I have a dream that one day even the state of Mississippi, a desert state, sweltering with the heat of injustice and oppression, will be transformed into an oasis of freedom and justice. I have a dream that my four children will one day live in a

nation where they will not be judged by the color of their skin but by the content of their character. I have a dream today.

—Martin Luther King, Jr. ("I Have A Dream" 1961)

By the way . . . Where did that quote about truth being self-evident come from?

Alliteration is a rhetorical device whereby one uses words with the same letter sounds to create sonorousness. This addition of a pleasing sound is not the only benefit to using alliteration. Like parallelism, it is a mnemonic device. Journalists, poets, politicians and clergy are just some of the professionals who employ alliteration to add pleasure and facilitate recollection of their ideas. In the text "Distracted," by Maggie Jackson, located in Chapter Seven, Jackson uses alliteration for this effect: "Of course, the news business has always been quick, fast and fueled by multitasking."

Euphemisms

People also struggle with *euphemisms*. Consider the ex-employee as she sits listening to a report on television about how some company, one similar to General Motors for which she had worked for twenty-five years, is "outsourcing." Why is she calling the television set names? She takes offense because she sees this as a euphemism, a method by which people make a negative act seem neutral or even positive. It sound disingenuous, dishonest. People become angry and frustrated and then they feel helpless when they perceive they are being bamboozled. They want to lash out against the people whom they perceive are behind the fuzzy language. So, let's not frustrate one another. Let's show a little respect for one another and speak directly and plainly. All we need to do is develop our critical thinking and then we can just let our logic and reason make whatever case we have to make for us. Let's treat one another with respect and not speak in *meaningless words*. What do you think of the quote below? Is it an example of "meaningless words" or a quote that has both a sense of sound and a sound of sense?

The best lack all conviction, while the worst
Are full of passionate intensity

—"The Second Coming" by W. B. Yeats

What Is Objective/Factual Language?

If some reference contains *objective language,* it has substance outside the mind of the speaker or listener. First, understand that the degree of objectivity one's words have in any given situation depends on the listener's ability to distinguish factual from nonfactual language. I consider myself fairly adept at this. Still, I can be confused.

Some people believe they have the "right" definition of "critical thinking," for example. They go so far as to research the origin of the word "critical." Some say it comes from the Greek word *krinein*, which means "to judge." Another author believes in the definition supplied by the Greek word *kriticos* and the Latin word *criticus*, which means "able to discern or separate." Even factual language, therefore, can cause problems. Are these translators trying to be objective? I suppose so, since they are using etymology to understand the original meaning. Do I get the same message from each of them? No. I have to use my experience and knowledge to define the word.

This is an example of the dilemma confronting all of us when observing language. After observing, we must *analyze*, which means to break down, make connections, ask questions. Is the word objective? Is it factual? Is it believable? It is the nature of language to be slippery. We must analyze vague words and try to clarify their meaning.

We can think of many such instances when authors or authorities seemed to be speaking objectively but were not entirely factual. They may have just misunderstood some faulty evidence, or their language may have been misleading, or both. I think we all must know that this sort of inaccurate speech can have serious consequences. The "error" in speech is not an excuse for a misinformed public.

Think of any history lesson you learned that eventually turned out to be wrong. Think of some statistic that you once believed to be indisputable. Better yet, think of some theory you have heard people postulating. We hear people discussing theories quite often on "news" channels and we might be convinced to believe that theories are reality. We should all question the news, and especially question "popular" speakers, those who put forward "discussions" using "authorities" as "news." Are there any solid facts? Any valid, qualified evidence offered as proof during these discussions? They may discuss possibilities. Are the people offering us their "opinions" informed, qualified authorities? Is this "news" information or entertainment?

Another situation during which we should question facts that are put forward by "authorities" is during history lessons taught differently by different texts and different teachers at different times. Look at these two versions about the same event:

"The Indians were slaughtered by the soldiers at Sand Creek."

"Five hundred twenty Native American men, women, and children were killed by soldiers at Sand Creek."

Subjective Language: Abstract Nouns

Abstract nouns refer to ideas or concepts; they have no *specific* physical referents as do the words "crayon," "Paris," or "Skype." While listening or reading, most people will not imagine, will not envision or hear the same thing, will not mentally recreate the same sensation or image. There are, of course, levels of abstraction. Some abstract nouns are more subjective than others. The abstract noun *loneliness* is emotionally charged and vague. It does not create an image which most of us would envision in the same way as we would from the word physical isolation.

We all use abstract nouns to generalize and convey ideas. They are a necessary part of our communication. As critical thinkers, we just need to be aware of when we might need to clarify them. That can be done by adding a specific adjective before the abstract noun.

Sometimes story writers want to reveal a character's psychological problem: "John knew what he had to do. He was sure that he could maintain control and that no one had control of him." The meaning would be clearer if the writer included *what kind of control:* "He was sure he could maintain physical control. . . ." Here, the specific adjective "physical" clarifies the meaning.

Sometimes professionals, authorities, generalize. This is an important, necessary part of their professions. Their abstract words have accepted definitions upon which their professional communities rely. The psychological term "Personality Disorder," as defined below by the 2015 Diagnostic and Statistical Manual (DSM-5), is abstract. As of 2015, professionals in the field of psychology have reached a consensus as to this definition.

> The Schizoid Personality Disorder is characterized by a pervasive pattern of social detachment and a restricted range of emotional expression. For these reasons, people with this disorder tend to be socially isolated. They don't seem to seek out or enjoy close relationships. They almost always chose solitary activities, and seem to take little pleasure in life. These "loners" often prefer mechanical or abstract activities that involve little human interaction and appear indifferent to both criticism and praise.

Concrete nouns refer to specific referents. Readers or listeners can imagine or envision the same thing, mentally recreate the sensation or the image. Adding adjectives that are specific to nouns, or selecting specific nouns makes our communication more clear. Rather than blame "the government" for high taxes, use a specific noun: "The IRS tax structure favors those who make over 250,000 per year." Tell someone you have a pet bird and they will want to know *what kind.* Why not choose the word "canary" at the outset?

However, as mentioned above, abstract words can be made more concrete with specificity.

If we were to use the word "addiction" in an article to the general public, rather than in an article, discussion or presentation for a psychology or other college course that had stipulated the definition of "addiction," we would want to qualify our meaning. For the general public, the word addiction is pretty vague. So, how could we make it more specific and concrete so that people could imagine it? We could define the abstract word with an example, of course: "Addiction to the Internet, spending more than five hours a day, every day, on dating or gaming sites, Facebook or other social media, ..." We can also just preface the abstract word with a one or two-word adjective: "Social media addiction . . ." The concept is clearer; it is still not perfectly clear, but it is less vague and broad. This is how we have to think of language, as having degrees or levels of generality or specificity, vagueness or clarity.

We can apprehend this phenomenon easily by picturing something we are familiar with, a number line.

Let's call ours "a language line." Where on the line should we place the words addiction, smoking habit and 2-pack-a-day cigarette smoking habit?

Abstract ————————————————————————————— Concrete

DISCUSSION 1.2

Here are three multiple choice questions to test your understanding of the difference between abstract and concrete nouns, vague and specific verbs or adjectives.

1. Which word in the below quote is the most abstract noun?

> Recent studies have revealed interesting types of addiction. Females and males use technology for different reasons. Women use cell phones and the Internet to connect socially. Men use cell phones and the internet to check on financial fluctuations in the stock market or to keep up with their school activities.

a. females

b. technology

c. fluctuations

d. addiction

2. Which verb is the most specific? Use the language line to help you gauge your answer.

Vague ─────────────────────────────── Specific

    a. keep up

    b. revealed

    c. use

    d. check on

3. Which adjective is the most specific?

Vague ─────────────────────────────── Specific

    a. recent

    b. interesting

    c. different

    d. financial

Other uses of this lesson: Research and source selection
Besides increasing our ability to speak, read and write with clarity, this language lesson will help those of you have been tasked with researching and selecting credible, informative sources. As you read articles for use as possible supports or analysis, you should consider the degree of objectivity or subjectivity, abstraction or concreteness, generality or specificity. Concrete nouns, specific adjectives and verbs and clearly defined abstract nouns will add objectivity and believability, credibility to the articles you are considering.

A Brief Word on Verbs and Adjectives (Objective vs. Subjective)

Verbs
You have probably considered, at this point, that more careful, reasonable thinking may produce more of the same kind of writing. I do understand that some of you may not be up on your language tools, especially grammar. Briefly, let me explain what verbs are and how they are used to convey fact (objectivity) or opinion (subjectivity).

Verbs are words that express action, ("run," "jog") existence ("is"), or occurrence ("suggest," "imply," "insinuate," "rely"). The action verbs are more obvious and objective. We can somewhat distinguish a run from a walk.

The inaction verbs are words like "is" or "seems" or "thinks." Verbs can be very powerful image makers. They can also easily sneak by our discerning sensors.

The police officer reports that the alleged perpetrator was witnessed to have been "fleeing" the gas station. What's wrong with this? He *was* fleeing you say? Okay. How do you know? Can you see "fleeing"? Such language is *slanted*, evidencing a negative or positive interpretation on the part of the speaker. Is it ever good to "flee"? Sure, but this word almost always implies an escape.

When trying to speak factually, try to show how this looks so anyone can *visualize* the action. What would be a more objective, exact word to use? The verb *sprinting* would be better.

"Fleeing" assumes that the runner is a perpetrator in the police report referenced above. The police officer has perhaps implied this person's guilt, has inferred that this person was indeed trying to escape because he was not, perhaps, standing, sitting, or walking outside the gas station.

Adjectives

Adjectives describe nouns. We use them to add detail:

> "What kind of sentence was it?" It was "a *life* sentence" or "a *fragmented part of* a sentence."

Adjectives give quality, quantity: blue, yellow, fat, skinny, rotund, honest and truthful, etc., are all adjectives. If you put the word or phrase before a noun and it describes or modifies the meaning of the noun, it is an adjective. The adjectives I have just employed as examples are abysmally inadequate. Objective adjectives would look like this: "He drew from his pocket a four-inch, double-bladed knife." See how specific the wording is? Adjectives should clarify the picture. If they don't "show" enough detail, if they are not explicit enough, they might mislead the reader/listener. You can make your language more credible, less vague, if you take out a thesaurus and find more concrete, specific, objective adjectives. Chapter Four of this text addresses this idea in more detail, but for now, consider: What does "baby blue" mean, as in, "The blanket was baby blue"? Babies who are blue are not healthy!

Also, when writing or speaking, use adjectives to qualify or quantify your meaning. Students should consider, before writing an essay on "drug addiction," the necessity to define the kind of drug and what addiction, an abstract noun, means. Physicians and psychologists differ as to their definition of addiction, and even lay people these days would most likely ask you to distinguish between "acute" and "chronic" addiction.

Frustration with themselves, not knowing how to respond, can cause people to sputter out things like "ridiculous" (or less socially acceptable language), and this does nothing but let their frustration out. Venting does little to help reasonable communication, because it just lets the other person know your feelings. That's okay, but if you leave it at that, you do not get anything solved. No one is telling you not to have feelings, but you should ask yourself, what do I get out of putting my feelings first, ahead of my brain? Try to see the big picture, the ultimate result you want in the long run. I think we parents have one very important advantage over our children, which also distinguishes an adult from a child, and that is the ability to see the big picture. Adults can more easily avoid getting caught up in the minor details and see instead what is truly at stake for him/herself and others in the long run.

SUSPENDING JUDGMENT

If you want to communicate effectively, you need to suspend judgment. One way to do this is to address your attention to a person's words, not to his/her personality or character. Focus on the language, not on the person. Try to not react to voice inflections. Ask: "What do I think the word means? What is causing my reaction? What associations with this language am I possibly making?"

Here's what I mean. Look at the difference between two conversations, versions A and B:

LOVER'S QUARREL (VERSION A)

Marilyn: You're a liar.
John: No, I'm not!
Marilyn: Yes, you are. You lied to me. You are a liar!
John: So are *you*. What about you? Remember that time . . .

This conversation, if you can call it that, has been cleaned up a bit. The word "liar" could be replaced by any number of labels that we hear all too often. We have all been negatively labeled before. Most of us don't like it. The word can hurt you, right? No. Wrong. It is a word. What power does it have? It has as much power as *you* give it. Again, one needs to see the big picture. We all can realize this type of conversation will go nowhere, or will indeed go down the drain, if John lets it. It will regress into more hurtful, less sophisticated language and end up hurting everyone and helping no one. Can you remember any conversation you had like this, one where hurtful words were dredged up to throw at the listener? Sure you can. Remember high school? Remember the first day of school? Better yet, remember those little sibling rivalry things you engaged in with your sister or brother? You must remember some verbal slugfest? Do you remember where it led? Where do you think this type of conversation will lead? It will probably degenerate, become irritated like an open wound. If you like that sort of thing, then put down this book. If you don't like your conversations like this, fear not. There is a way to stop it, to stop the progress of irrational, emotional messages from festering. You need to think about language. I know. This sounds difficult. Well, it is! But it pays off. Just look below and see the difference, in version B, when we apply a simple, reasonable approach to communicating. John, the husband below, observes Marilyn's language:

VERSION B:

Marilyn: You're a liar.
   John: What do you mean by "liar"?

Okay? Do you see what I mean? One conversation has room for communication of something beyond raw emotion. Which version will open the door for discussion? What does the question do to limit, add reasoning, and control the conversation?

Here you see John asking for definition after he "observes" Marilyn's language. This is one skill we will learn to develop in order to prohibit arguments from getting out of hand. The question creates some emotional distance between John and Marilyn so that they can try to reason. (Let's just assume here that John wants to communicate because he does want to stay married.)

Admittedly, it's not the best or the only way to stop the disease of miscommunication from spreading, but you have to admit, it does something on the positive side. It at least stops her attack, albeit probably only temporarily. There's probably more persistent observing and defining to be done here. But now at least the illness is in remission. John has gained *some* control so that they can continue on to speak reasonably. Sometimes we need to let go of our tendency to control in order to really control our conversations. The above approach requires John to detach, to mentally distance himself from his impulse to fight back. He must observe what she is saying. It also entails asking for *clarification.* John is asking for what we will later learn is Marilyn's *premise,* specifically a premise based on need for *definition.* He wants to know what she means, what basis she has for her allegation. He thus avoids the tendency to be defensive and use the "you also" type of argument, better known as "I know you are, but what am I?" He knows that type of arguing is childish. You will learn how to voice acceptable premises and use/ask for definition as you read further. No one can reason with another person about anything that is to any degree complex without these skills.

Of course, there are a few people who will try to use definition to manipulate, and possibly distract people, get them away from the issue. If you are a critical thinker, you will not allow this, and will be able to keep the discussion focused on the pursuit of truth. First, you need to practice analyzing language.

Observing over a period of time and making a conscious choice to slow down and observe just the facts of a graphic or a text, requires discipline and is not learned overnight. What follows is a lesson that will develop your patience and self-discipline while reading and thinking critically. Let's go to the language lessons.

LANGUAGE LESSON 1: What is language analysis?

1: Automatic Expression (Auto) vs. Considered, Reasonable Thought (CRT)

Whenever people ask me what distinguishes a non-critical thinker from a critical thinker, I explain that a non-critical thinker is not so much concerned with the fairness and accuracy of his/her statements as automatically *expressing* whatever is on his mind and in his heart; the critical thinker considers the issue at hand, thinks before speaking and articulates a *considered, reasonable thought* that is based on something tangible or factual. The non-critical thinker might not even care if the other person hears, thinks or responds. His purpose is to express, let out his emotions. People who speak on automatic pilot don't tend to care about inviting others into a reasonable discussion based on something objective, and don't consider whether there might be disagreement or uncertainty on the part of the other person or persons. The critical thinker does care, sometimes very much. Why? We want to be satisfied with the way we are communicating, learning, developing our ideas and feel secure that we are understanding other like, serious-minded people so as to perhaps reach some consensus and further our knowledge, sharpen or broaden our perspectives or perfect our approaches or methodologies.

A couple of examples will help you see the difference between expression and reasoning:

Automatic Expression:
A. "I know for a fact that there is no supreme being (1) and we are all alone in this world (2). That's why we must all be self-sufficient (3)."

Considered, Reasonable Thought:
B. "Because it is possible that there is no supreme being (1), we should make an effort (2) to be responsible and control what we can in our own, individual daily lives (3)."

What is the main difference between statements A and B? It might seem like an easy question to answer, but can you answer it so another reasonable person can see the basis for your reasoning? This isn't as easy as it sounds. It requires analysis of the wording I have underlined.

Recognizing an unfounded and unreasonable statement is one thing; explaining to another person why you think the statement doesn't make sense, providing the objective basis of your assessment is something else. When engaging in conversation at your place of business, conversation that is about business, or responding to a text or speech in college work, academic papers, class discussions, some language analysis is required, at least if you want to get beyond the basics, so that you can join in a serious, responsible business or academic discourse. Taking apart, separating out one set of words from another is called *language analysis*.

What follows is a set of practice questions designed to be discussed with others. Share your answers and explanations with others. Listen to their explanations for their answers as well.

DISCUSSION 1.3

First, here are statements A and B again:

Automatic Expression:

A. "<u>I know for a fact that there is no supreme being (1)</u> and <u>we are all alone in this world</u> (2). <u>That's why we must all be self-sufficient. (3)</u>."

B. "<u>Because it is possible that there is no supreme being (1)</u>, <u>we should make an effort (2)</u> to be <u>responsible and control what we can in our own, individual daily lives (3)</u>."

STATEMENT A

1. Consider only statement A. Is the overall tone inviting you to think? Do you hear any *pathos appeal* (appeal to emotion)? Try taking apart the wording, questioning the language: what words stand out? Are they personal or impersonal? Consider types of verbs, nouns, and adjectives as you respond.

2. How would you describe the tone? To which words (choose 1, 2 or 3) can you tie this tone?

3. Could the assertions, any of them, be supported with facts or evidence? (consider 1, 2 and 3). Is STATEMENT A AUTO or CRT? Explain your reasoning.

STATEMENT B

4. Which of the underlined phrases (1, 2 or 3) will most likely invite discussion? Explain as reasonably as you can by considering ONLY the language, not your personal experiences.

5. Which of the underlined phrases (1, 2 or 3) could be supported by facts and/or evidence? Explain as reasonably as you can by considering only the language, not your personal experiences.

6. Which two words appeal to logos (logic)? Is STATEMENT B AUTO or CRT?

Having some trouble discerning AUTO from CRT? Explain what is giving you difficulty:

_____

_____

The first statement, STATEMENT A, is an expression or assertion of ones unfounded, unsupported and unsupportable opinion. How do we know this? Ask yourself, would you really argue with that statement? Why not? Not easy to explain. Start here: could you present objective facts or evidence rather than personal testimony to support the ideas expressed there?

How to Strengthen Language Analysis Skills

In order to analyze language effectively and use our language analysis to explain why an argument or statement is or is not reasonable, we have to learn some terms for language. So, let's start with some basic terms and see just how easy it really is to analyze language: **hyperbolic, qualified and slanted language** are all kinds of language you already notice; you just might not have the terms for them.

In STATEMENT A, the speaker introduces the declaration of fact without inclusion of a fact: "I know for a fact" and the exaggeration inherent in the words "no supreme being" and then we have the exaggerated exclamation "all alone in this world."

Also in STATEMENT A, the speaker uses the word "all" twice, once in each sentence. We will analyze such phrasing soon, but for now, keep in mind this first example of exaggerated language or *hyperbole*. We are all allowed to express our opinions. But how does exaggerating help facilitate discussion?

The second statement, STATEMENT B, is more reasonably worded: "Because it is possible that there is no supreme being, we should make an effort to be responsible and control what we can in our own lives." Sure, it is an opinion as well, yet it is a supported and *qualified* opinion. The appeal is logical, known as logos appeal. Not that we can see the evidence there in the sentence. There is no factual support evident. However, we do see a basis of reasoning (Because. . .). We will expect this assertion to be supported by causal reasoning.

The word "because" causes us to expect the speaker will be giving us what we will later call a *premise, a basis for reasoning.*

Additionally, the second statement avoids exaggeration (hyperbole) by using the **qualifier** "possible;" the speaker is not asserting an *absolute* (100% for certain, "we are *all* alone in the world") that leaves no room for discussion. Instead, our speaker leaves open a *possibility* (which allows the other person to participate and question, offer his/her ideas as to what you think is possible: "Because it is *possible* that there is no supreme being, we should make an effort to be responsible and control what we can in our own lives." Other **qualifiers** like "some" or "occasionally" or "sometimes" (rather than always) are helpful as well.

LANGUAGE LESSON 2: SLANTING

There are three ways of slanting a discussion: slanted language, labeling and omitting relevant information.

Slanting

We all want to get what we want. We want sometimes to make or even force others to think the way we think, want what we do, say what we want them to say and even believe what we think is right to believe. In an effort to fulfill our desires, we sometimes choose language that is more emotional than thoughtful. We call this **slanted language**. *Slanted language* is language that has been selected to convey an author's beliefs or opinions and hopefully modify another person's perspective on any given subject.

We hear slanted language in advertising and political speeches. Some words all by themselves are heavily slanted. Slanted language is language that has a flavor to it; it is not neutral, or mostly neutral on a scale of 1–10, and so is likely to evoke some positive or negative association and feeling. There is plenty of slanted language that is familiar, especially in advertising and the political sphere. In common conversations, it can have unintended consequences, create a negative or positive reaction we had not anticipated. Why?

Because we speak and hear thousands of words everyday, we don't think about them. It's like water. We use it; what's to think about? But wait: how many times have you been offended by something someone said only to get the excuse "I didn't mean it"? Sure, we can't control how everyone is going to react to everything we say, but we can get some control by learning to recognize different types of words.

As you become more aware of different types of language and make more considered, logical and conscious choices when you speak or write, <u>you will feel more in control of your communications</u>. To some extent you do this already. We all do, for example when we worry about the political correctness of our speech. But there is more to it than just speaking in generalities or *euphemisms.*

You are probably pretty well aware of one phenomenon that results from overuse of certain slanted language: people tune out. The slanted language meant to persuade, to turn someone else towards or away from something or someone actually might have the opposite effect: people might very well just stop listening or they might become overly energized, like some of the people this political season (2012) whom have become quite agitated about health care.

Carefully chosen slanted language can be very effective for getting away with things, praising or hurting people, causing calm or unrest. When we choose words that have some sting or positive or negative weight, we make the communication uneven. We are not thinking critically when we choose such words. We are reacting emotionally. Critical thinkers need to stay detached, neutral, and avoid the impulse to slant.

Sometimes we choose words that we hope will call up a certain association and then associate that word with a person or organization or group so as to affect the listening or reading audience.

Slanting by Omitting
This occurs when we leave out relevant information. We just give part of the story, the part we want heard for our own reasons.

Two Examples:

1. The Republican says: "Don't vote for Ms. Taylor. Ms. Taylor voted four times for Democrats!" (leaving out that she voted 12 times for Republicans.)

2. On Monday Harold says: "Mom, Coach Cortes made me run around the track three times more than everyone else today!" (leaving out the reason for this, which was that Harold had skipped practice three times the previous week.)

In the above two examples, we can see another type of slanting at work: *slanting by omitting.* If we want to skew someone's perception of another person, event or situation, we can accomplish this pretty easily by omitting information that would point out the positive.

Unlike the objective language we have studied, language that is more or less neutral and factual even out of context (words that are objective, like numbers, dates, times, measurements, directions, etc.) slanted language is subjective. I will discuss the neutral, factual language some more later. For now, try to recall some argument you heard or were engaged in that contained subjective, exaggerated language, even a negative slant or tone. Think back. Don't just consider what another person said but what you said. Yes, you do it too. So do I. We get into arguments and select out or "omit" information or facts that don't fit our current purposes and sometimes we throw in some hyperbole to boot:

"You always drink all the milk."

is slanted language (*hyperbole*) and slanting by omission of pertinent information.

"You never take me anywhere."
"But I do. I did. I . . ."
"Nope. Never, anywhere."

What can we do? Well, for starters, don't argue with that. You can't, not reasonably. Instead, you can try to steer it back to a more neutral, reasonable tone and ask questions and see if you can coax out a concession: "What makes you think that? Isn't that a little extreme?"

For those of you who are making those accusations: What hope is there for a reasonable discussion when you're accusing someone of always doing something, especially *always* drinking *all* the milk or never taking you anywhere?

Another type of Slanting: Labeling

Label makers want to accomplish one thing above all else, and it's not critical thinking. Label makers want you instantly to accept a connection between the two things, the label and the person/situation or thing that is being labeled. Not all labels are bad. We need labels for types of food and beverages, for example. Don't we need labels for people too? Well, maybe. Let's think about it. First, labeling oversimplifies, makes us weak thinkers. "He is an x so he is not a y." See? Simple. No thought necessary and end of discussion. Second, labeling takes away another person's individuality. Yes, we all have individuality and we should cherish that.

Third, it avoids the **question at issue**, redirects a conversation away from solving the actual problem and again, subverts the person's individual identity.

DISCUSSION 1.4

1. What are two labels for groups of people which you find particularly objectionable?

2. Discuss why you find them objectionable. Why do you think people use these labels?

EXERCISES 1A–D FOR CHAPTER ONE

EXERCISE 1A

Below are five sentences with italicized phrases for you to consider in light of what you have just studied. Read the sentences and choose whether the *italicized phrases* help make the meaning **A**. exaggerated or absolute; **B**. qualified and partially reasonable or **C**. mostly reasonable.

1. *Some people* are not aware of the dangers of secondhand smoke.
   A   B   C

2. *There is some evidence, from both sides of the gun control debate*, that handguns are involved in this country.   **A   B   C**

3. In *the last thirty years*, the public and law enforcement working together *have made some progress in curtailing the number of rapes* in Center City. *We might be able to* bring down the number of rape incidents to *below a dozen by 2011.*   **A   B   C**

4. *All of these scientists, these priests of evolution*, would have you *worship science* rather than the holy word of our Almighty God.   **A   B   C**

5. *We have* to save our country. *We need* change. *We know* what will happen if we let these people take over. *They don't want* to help out the little guy. *They don't care* about you or your grandma. Shoot. These are the same types of guys that ran Enron, and they'll run our country into the ground just like they did!   **A   B   C**

EXERCISE 1B ANALYZE LANGUAGE

Which of the below contains hyperbole? Where do you see qualifiers? How about a euphemism? Do you see subjective adjectives or labeling? Underline and use these abbreviations to identify: H = hyperbole; Q = qualifiers; E = euphemism; SA for subjective adjective ; and L for labeling.

                                                                H
EX: How can we take a guy like Tom Brown seriously? <u>Everybody knows</u>
           L
he's a <u>tree hugging liberal.</u>

1. We all know George has had a hard time since he lost his parents.

2. George used to always complain about his family.

3. Now, there are some times when he wishes he could have them back, especially his mother.
4. George was closer to his mother than he was to his father.
5. He blamed his father for their dysfunctional family.

EXERCISE 1C WRITE 3 PARAGRAPHS

Find an article or story by a writer (novelist, short story writer), a blogger, a politician or advertiser that shows label making. Summarize the text, giving your reader the main points and overall purpose, as you see it, of the text. Who is labeled? How? What is the effect, do you think, of this label making on the person or persons labeled and the label maker himself? Are some labels necessary? It does not have to be a "negative label." Write the answers to the above questions and more; don't confine yourself to just those initial questions. Share your thoughts on labeling in this article or story or blog and then in general, showing your ability to apply the above language analysis lessons, in 3 paragraphs. Be sure to give the title of the webpage or article, the date you viewed, the date the piece was published, and who published it.

EXERCISE 1D

Describe what you can see in each of the photos on the facing page, Melancholy and Sweet Clouds. Write two paragraphs. Describe in objective language so that someone who had never seen these photos could fairly well picture them. Use concrete nouns, specific adjective and verbs. After this, imagine a context for the photos. Where is this? What has happened?

Photo by Mirabelle Jones

Photo by Mirabelle Jones

CHAPTER TWO

Distinguishing Fact from Opinion

To distinguish fact from opinion, we first have to try to understand why our brains might fail to make the distinction at one time or another. Here are some common mistakes that we all make that impede our ability to think reasonably. I have, of course, provided some tentative solutions at the end of each section.

First we should all acknowledge a common phenomenon: People sometimes think that others mean harm when in fact they may indeed be innocent of any intention to harm. This is known as *reading between the lines*.

People assume they know other people's intentions. This occurs quite often in the workplace. An employee assumes that his boss is "out to get him" when his boss asks about the progress on some particular piece of work:

> **Boss:** Did you get that report typed up yet?
> **Employee:** I've been working as hard as I can on it. I even worked through lunch yesterday!
> **Boss:** Did you get that report typed up yet?

What happened here? The boss asked if the report had been typed yet. The employee heard a personal, negative criticism. People also do this kind of thing with friends and loved ones. Just look at this next example and see if this sounds familiar:

> **Mother:** Do you need help with your homework?
> **Daughter:** Why are you always criticizing me? I'm not stupid!
> **Mother:** I am *not* criticizing you. I'm just offering to—
> **Daughter:** You are too! I told you that the only reason I got that stupid D in algebra was because I missed the test on that day I was sick.
> **Mother:** I didn't say anything about your being stupid.
> **Daughter:** You did too, and you know it!

Mother: What did I say?
Daughter: Oh, forget it! Leave me alone.

We care most for these particular people (even though they seem to be trying to drive us crazy), and our lives can even center on them. We are most involved and sometimes dependent on them, and therefore more likely to think we know what these people are *really saying.* We don't *listen for factual language,* but instead start early on in the conversation to form opinions as to the "real" meaning behind the words.

This can become a habit. So, why does this kind of miscommunication happen? Are we all just trying to misunderstand and be misunderstood? Such a habit can lead to a feeling of isolation. The child above probably does feel very alone.

Misinterpreting happens for many reasons. We let one word connect to another without questioning the connections. We make associations too quickly. What can we do to try to avoid this mistake, a mistake that can have irrevocable consequences?

We can stop ourselves, count to ten, and think: "Hey, wait a minute. Does that word really mean what I think it means?" Words fly by too fast. Someone needs to say, "Please. I don't understand. Slow down."

Look at the example below:

Wife: You seem to have a hard time listening to me.
Husband: No. I'm listening to you.

This is usually not a reassuring response to a complaint that one is not listening. Instead, the person accused of not listening should ask, "What makes it *seem* like I'm not listening?" For whatever reason, the other person thinks that is an issue. It should be discussed.

Another reason people fail to interpret reasonably and responsibly, to ask for *definition,* is that they are impatient, so they cut one another off. They think they know what others are about to say. Here again, reading between the lines causes poor communication. Some people think they can see the future. (There are prophets all around us.) Thinking too quickly, thinking in a panicky or stressful state, is how I would define this "impatience." It causes people to talk over one another. Mechanics try this tactic on me. I don't care why they do it. I just make them stop. "Hold it," I say. "Let's slow down and discuss what you mean by my engine is *broken.*"

Another mistake occurs when we "see" only what we want to see, as opposed to what is actually there. Jean Paul Sartre, an eminent twentieth century

French philosopher, proposed the idea of "bad Faith." We may know this as "looking through rose-colored glasses." We can apply this to our language lesson by considering again what we noted in Chapter One: We all have been guilty of misreading what to most people would probably be considered a pretty clear message.

Almost every day, those of us energetic enough to escape the soft, warm glow of the television screen venture out into the world and are immediately bombarded by images that we have to interpret. We see our cars, our keys, our gas gauges. As in the case above, where we don't listen to the language of others, here too we avoid paying attention to what is right in front of us. We misinterpret. In this case, we are speaking to ourselves, a silent, internal language. We "observe" facts and then interpret, or misinterpret: "Gas gauge. Needle below red part. Hmm. I can make it. It's only a *little* below the red line. I've made it before on that much gas."

(Before we go further, let's all agree. The gas gauge on this car works just fine. Okay, let's go on to interpret our observation.)

You and I know what the gas needle probably indicates. The driver above may *know* too. So, when the car runs out of gas on the freeway, what caused it? It wasn't the set of facts that were readily apparent. It certainly wasn't what was observable. The car needed gas.

We all do this kind of thing at times, skew or *slant* the truth; in romantic situations, during family disputes, we adjust the facts, omit some information.

The key to stopping these acts of "bad Faith" is to be aware of what we are saying or doing and the *possible* or *probable* effects. At some point, we should replay the scene, view what we have done, listen to what we have said, and consider the possibility that we could have been mistaken, possibly fooling ourselves. We continue to run out of gas on the freeway only when we fail to acknowledge our mistaken, faulty, or *fallacious* thinking.

Fallacious, faulty reasoning can also occur when we ascribe credibility to someone's testimony just because he/she seems like an authority.

People tend to see what experts tell them to see. ("You can see by this photo that this man is feeling guilty.") We don't scrutinize documents and/ or question so-called facts an "expert" offers us. We might sign things without reading the fine print because someone assures us that it is legitimate. Such careful reading and thinking about what we are reading is supposedly unnecessary: "That would take too much time, and besides, I can trust what this man is saying," my niece said to me three months ago when she bought a fifteen-year-old car. You can guess where that car is now. Let's face it: It's easier to trust people when you need something from them. That's where they get you, if you let them. That's when you really need to turn up the volume on your "voice of reason."

Is That a Fact? What Is a Fact?

"Facts, facts, facts, facts. I *hate* facts!" (My son at age nine.)

It is incredibly difficult to explain to some people that there are things called "facts." This is how you do it. Consider:

1. Facts can be observed. They exist outside your interpretation of them, outside of your judgments or your values for them. They are independent of you.
2. Factual statements are not just opinions. A statement of fact would not include opinionated words.
3. Facts can be proven by evidence.
4. A fact is either present or there is a trace that the thing or event did once exist. Did Iraq have "weapons of mass destruction" present from late 2002 to early 2003? Some evidence could verify this in order to make a positive assertion credible.

There are many historical examples of people doubting facts the majority of us feel we just know are definitely facts. For instance, some Europeans, from 1943–45, did not believe the Holocaust happened. Think about it. How did they come to believe the Holocaust did in fact occur? How did they come to believe the facts? Some people today argue as to the degree of "global warming" or as it is now called "climate change." Senator Inhofe has scientists that he relies on. The IPCC (Intergovernmental Panel on Climate Change) has scientists that they rely on. Is one set of facts more verifiable than another? Is some evidence more supportable, more valid? Do the qualifications and experience of the experts matter? Sure they do.

DISCUSSION 2.1

When we choose sources to support a position, provide evidence for an argument paper, we should look for facts. Of course, there will be some subjective or some abstract language. Unless the document is just a statistical analysis or report, we will expect to see a blend of subjective and objective language. Still, the article we choose should, overall, be mostly analytical and neutral in tone.

For example, say we have been assigned to write a research paper. We have been tasked to conduct research and choose an article to support the position that in 2014, women do not have economic parity in the workplace. Which of the below paragraphs should you consider as the most reliable, A or B? Discuss the specific reasons for your answer.

A. The Organization for Economic Development reports that women are still not achieving at the same rate as men. Only about 15 percent of women hold positions on corporate boards. It gets even more dismal when you look further, below the board level.

B. According to the U.S. Department of Labor Statistics (2014), 57 percent of women between the ages of 21–65 in the United States are in the workforce. Their median weekly earnings are $719 per week. The median weekly earnings for males is $871 per week. This considers full-time workers who worked year round, including those who are self-employed.

Using Authorities for Factual Support/Evidence

Some audiences accept credible or multiple witness testimony. Others accept the testimony of authorities. Belief in an authority's testimonial *evidence* again depends on the audience and their experiences. It also depends on the credibility of the witness or authority. Authorities need to *qualify* themselves somehow, usually by education and experience. Dr. James Smith gives your mother advice on her cancer therapy. Ask the doctor what his specialty is, where he went to school, what degrees, licenses, experience he has, etc., in order to *qualify* him.

When you read a factual article, always look for a statement of purpose somewhere, usually at the beginning or the end. Look at the title and see if there is any *slanted language*. We would consider language that conveys opinion slanted. Also, consider the source before trying to assess if the language is possibly slanted, even though the words may appear factual. For whom does this person work? What are his/her political or religious affiliations? Does he/she seem to be appealing to a certain audience? Are some facts omitted that might or might not appeal to a female, gay, wealthy, elderly audience?

Sometimes the sheer number of authorities has more evidentiary value. This was the case when it came to the Holocaust mentioned above. Some say this was the case in the first Menendez brothers murder trial in California in the early 1990s. These brothers, who had admittedly killed their parents, presented several authorities who claimed that the "boys," both legally adults, had been sexually abused and terrorized by their father. The experts appealed to the sympathies of the jury. Yes, the brothers had purchased guns under a false ID and did shoot their parents (who were sitting on the living room sofa eating strawberries). Still, they almost avoided a murder charge. Several authorities testified as to the abuse the "boys" had suffered at the hands of their parents. Ultimately, reason prevailed. If you or I use authority in writing to support our point, we should probably use more than one. However, we should be careful about giving weight to authorities' abilities to provide relevant, factual evidence concerning cause and effect, or motive.

EYEWITNESS TESTIMONY

Besides testimony from authorities, we must carefully consider and question eyewitness testimony. Eyewitness testimony is the least reliable type of testimony. The testimony of someone who claims to have seen or otherwise received relevant sensory information regarding an event or object should be questioned thoroughly. Significant problems may arise as we consider the validity and accuracy of such testimony. First, the witness, let's call her Belinda, may not have a clear recollection of the events for a variety of reasons. This can result in faulty testimony if she claims to have a clear recollection, testifies she is positive she saw/heard/smelled something. She might have a clear recollection but alas might lack the verbal ability to accurately convey her recollection. What might make that condition lead to even more distorted testimony would be the rare case where the person taking down the testimony *leads* the witness, ("puts words in her mouth"). Of course, there is always the possibility that Belinda does have verbal ability and chooses to lie, to embellish, or to diminish some facet of her recollection (select/omit/slant the truth) because of some bias.

> **Attorney:** "Belinda, did you actually see the man run down the stairs at 5:55 that morning?"
> **Belinda:** "Yes, absolutely. He was fleeing the scene and trying to make off with that poor old woman's piggy bank."

Such problems with eyewitness testimony are well known to lawyers and judges.

PHYSICAL EVIDENCE

Of course, physical evidence, to be considered in any situation, should be shown to be relevant and must be verified and authenticated as to its origin. Where was it found? How old is it? Is it in its original shape? In whose possession has it been in the last x amount of time? Could it be a copy? Physical evidence, observed and verified by scientists is still not considered 100% absolute evidence that x happened exactly as someone has said it did.

Scientists, people who conduct experiments after positing hypotheses, can only come to a consensus, a consensus (agreement) as to how something probably occurred. Investigators of crimes likewise must process information, rather than just rely on testimony or a couple of pieces of evidence. After processing, questioning, doubting, running more tests, comparing and contrasting and eliminating what is least likely, they come to some conclusions. The nice thing about this kind of fact/evidence-based reasoning is the scientist or investigator or anyone that conducts such careful evidence gathering and scrutinizing can retrace his/her steps, showing us just how the results were obtained.

Again, ask questions of your "evidence" before offering it as support for your case and ask questions regarding the evidence others proffer for your acceptance. Critical thinkers don't assume and don't take anything or anyone at face value when it comes to "evidence" and they always have ready some method of validating their evidence.

Can We Rely on Statistics as *Evidence*?

Statistics are usually fact-based. Some statistics, like those on a sports page, use only numbers and observations that many people can verify. These are pretty valid and provoke few questions as to their reliability. Sometimes statistics are based on studies. Statistics are not necessarily factual, but they are often used as *evidence*. Even the U.S. Census Bureau will admit that. And yes, even they will admit there is a margin of error.

Studies require qualification. You must research studies and statistics based on them in order to prove that they represent factual *evidence* of something, to be sure that the people doing the study are qualified and that you can qualify the information for your reader. How was the study done? Who participated? Who did not participate? Who conducted the study? When was it done? Where was it done? How long was it conducted? These and other questions need to be researched and answered before a statistic based on a study is considered valid evidence. Be careful when citing statistical evidence. Be ready to back it up, somehow.

Studies based on surveys and polls are questionable. Let's say a poll claims that drug use among teenagers is leveling off and more teenagers are rejecting the idea that drugs are cool. Their survey apparently shows that 35 percent of teens felt that "most people will try marijuana sometime," down from 40 percent a year ago.

Discuss this with others. What, if anything, do you think is wrong with such a survey, and this survey in particular, insofar as its ability to tell the truth and present "facts"? Try to think of at least three questions you would like to ask the pollsters.

Read the article titled "Distracted" by Maggie Jackson, located in Chapter Seven. She is a Professor of the Social Studies of Science and Technology in the Program in Science, Technology, and Society at MIT (Massachusettes Institute of Technology). How does she support her points? Are her examples "expert testimony"? Is some of her language subjective? Does she provide some facts or evidence that you would consider reliable?

What Is an Opinion?

Opinions are not the facts themselves, and they are not evidence. They are sometimes based on what is believed to be factual, what seems to be true, but they are unproven. Yes, there are "expert" opinions, but some are not so valuable. Opinions are sometimes conclusions. They may be illogical *inferences*, which are conclusions drawn from evidence, on the basis of some perceived, accepted reality. Such conclusions, sometimes voiced at the beginning of a discussion, sometimes surmised after listing several things one believes, can cause heated arguments that don't result in any closure or mutual understanding. As critical thinkers, we want to perpetuate understanding. So, it is important that we have solid, evidentiary support for our opinions and avoid drawing illogical inferences.

I asked a student what he thought of his vocabulary. He replied, "It sucks." That was his opinion. At that moment, I came to share his opinion. So did the class. We laughed. They drew an *inference*, a conclusion based on the evidence he presented. His own language ("It sucks") allowed the class to agree with his opinion about his own vocabulary.

Opinions, to be seriously considered, should be based in fact, soundly rooted in an objective premise. The opinions of critical thinkers should be phrased objectively.

Likewise, when asking a person for his/her opinion, the question should not be a "leading" one, as they say in courtrooms where witnesses are being questioned. It all depends on how the question is phrased. Never ask," So, when did you stop beating your wife?" to start out with. Don't imply a fact not in evidence when asking a question.

Americans are raised to think that their opinions are valuable. They are also raised to value freedom of speech. Put the two together, without any other qualifications for expressing an opinion, and you get a lot of people shooting their mouths off in this great country of ours. People tune in to TV programs that allow them to hear other people's opinions. I believe these opinions are often viewed as "entertainment." Unfortunately, opinions that become absorbed without critical analysis soon lose their entertainment value when they are expressed in serious, important discussions. Standing around the water cooler at work, people begin to spout unproven assertions as facts, based on what they heard on the John O'Flannegan show. These same people like to go online and express their opinions on one of the several polls that are put up for our amusement. People tend to go along with the popular opinion; they tend to value majority opinion regardless of whether or not the opinion is based on facts. They tend to quickly "weigh in" so that their vote counts, so they "have a say" and are just as influential as the others, they think. People tend to not slow down, analyze and question the wording or the facts, if any, behind the question.

The few polls that I have seen online have been, shall we say, interestingly worded. The pollsters ask questions in what I would consider "leading" manners. Words that are not objective, factual and even highly slanted are sometimes used. Here is my version of a poorly worded, misleading and ineffective opinion poll.

What do you think? See the word violent below? Isn't that an abstract word?

Question: What do you think causes school shootings?

Fractured family life	9768	40.0%
Violent images in the media	2930	12.0%
Guns, weapons	2490	10.2%
Poor school attendance	3663	15.0%
Broken homes	2442	10.0%
Troubled youths who needed help	2442	10.0%
Other	726	3.0%
Total vote	24,461	

EXERCISES 2A–D FOR CHAPTER TWO

EXERCISE 2A

Write below three facts you found on the internet, facts, not statistics. Be sure to record somewhere where you got the information and the date you accessed it. Explain; why do you believe these are facts?

1. _____
2. _____
3. _____

EXERCISE 2B

1. Write below three statistics you found on the internet. Example: 43% of the reported victims of burglary in California were female.

2. Explain whether or not you believe the statistic is factual and credible and say why.

3. Give the url and the date you accessed the information.

Try Bureau of Justice Statistics http://bjs.ojp.usdoj.gov/index.cfm?ty=abu, the Bureau of Labor Statistics, ProQuest or your college library's Academic Search Premier, the FBI's website, the International Panel on Climate Change (IPCC) or National Oceanic and Atmospheric Administration (NOAA) the American Medical Association (AMA), maybe?

1. _____
2. _____
3. _____

EXERCISE 2C

Cite an opinion poll. State who conducted the poll, when and how. What inference do you draw from the poll? **Be sure to record where you got the information and the date you accessed it.**

_____
_____
_____

EXERCISE 2D

You will need to read a report or science article (not an editorial or blog) on-line regarding climate change in order to complete this exercise

1. What is the date on the report or science article and what is the name of the author(s) and title of the report you read? How many pages did you read? What is the url?

   _____

   _____

2. What was the purpose of the report? Who commissioned it?

   _____

   _____

3. Quote three factual statements.

   _____

   _____

4. Quote one statement that you think might be an example of slanting and explain why, applying language lessons from Chapters 1 and 2.

   _____

   _____

CHAPTER THREE

Stated and Unstated Premises

To understand what is logical, you need to understand what makes a statement illogical. At the root of most illogical thinking, if you dig long enough for it, you will probably find a faulty premise or two.

What is a premise? A *premise* is a general, foundational belief in a fact or a value. It is some general truth upon which people base their opinions and conclusions when arguing a position or making a proposal. A premise is just a *claim* of fact or value, a basis for a conclusion; it does not have to be true, but is rather just accepted by the author as a given. The audience will then choose to accept it or not.

When we hear a proposal, we should consider what premises the proposal takes for granted.

Example 1—Birth Control

If I propose that birth control of any sort should be legal, I must hold certain premises.

My position must be logically based upon some beliefs. I must:

1. believe birth can be controlled;

2. believe birth control methods are available; and

3. consider it is okay to try controlling conception.

All of these are premises I must hold before I launch into an argument for birth control. If I believe in a god that controls all things, in other words, some notion of "fate," I will have problems defending my argument for birth control. That would affect my premise #1, at least.

Hopefully you can see that these are broad, general beliefs. The first two are claims of fact, while the third is a value statement that relates to morality. If I believe in orthodox Catholicism, I'm definitely not going to agree with premise three. That would go against traditional Catholic morality. Premises are powerful.

Our basic American values are premises: "All men are created equal" is an opinion upon which I could base my argument for civil rights. It is a claim of value, an opinion, a premise. In Chapter 7 of this text, you will see the Declaration of Independence. Read it. Upon what premises does the author base his thesis, that people in the 13 states should declare independence from England? What is the factual basis? Can you see any claims of fact? How about conditional statements?

People *draw inferences* from premises. In the Declaration of Independence, you will see statements that follow the formula, "If one does x, it means y." There are some basic assumptions, of course, about the reader too. We can see that the writer assumes the reader (King George) is familiar with the historical accounts to which the writer refers: "He has called together legislative bodies at places unusual, uncomfortable, and distant from the depository of their Public Records." Will King George accept this premise as worded? Most likely not!

Not all premises are so clearly stated. Sometimes they are hidden. To discern what premise or assumption is hidden underneath a position statement or proposition, we must do some processing of the *question at issue*. "Upon what grounds does the speaker, or writer, base his/her argument?" we should ask.

We can all become confused when listening to another's assertions. An *assertion* is just a fact or opinion put forward; a premise is the foundation of an argument.

We all arrive at premises through life experience or learning. A president of a country may argue for a new law based on a premise that is factual. For example, knowing that cloning of stem cells is possible (a factual premise), she could go on to argue that cloning of stem cells from embryos is immoral, based on her premise that embryos are "live human beings." Her next step would be her conclusion: "Stem cell cloning should be outlawed." Note the word "should" indicates a *conclusion*, not a premise.

Your interlocutor, the person with whom you are communicating, may state premises. If a premise is stated, you can pretty much just accept it or not. If you don't hear or see an *acceptable premise*, and just hear a conclusion, a position or proposal statement, you should not proceed to argue the issue. You must inquire as to the person's premise.

Conclusions are not premises. Premises are the foundations of the argument. Conclusions are the results based on consideration of one's beliefs in fact or value. Words like "need" and "should" indicate a conclusion or *inference*, *a conclusion based on evidence*. Such words would logically not be present in a premise.

Example 2—Uncovering Premises

If a politician believes the United States armed forces *should* invade Iraq to make the people of the United States safer, you will recognize a proposal statement, a conclusion this politician has drawn. Now, consider: Upon what opinions, beliefs in fact or value, might this person be basing his/her opinion?

The next step to uncover the politician's premises is to start asking some objectively stated, reasonable questions:

"Do you believe there are weapons of mass destruction in Iraq, and that these might be used to attack a city in the United States?"

If the person answers yes, then probe further revealing the reasoning behind the assertion. How does this person define "weapons of mass destruction?" What might cause Iraq to use these weapons against the United States? You should also ask the person to define any words in his/her subsequent replies that are abstract or vague, in your estimation. Language plays a big role in this, as does cause/effect reasoning. Asking questions, related to the nouns and verbs, the significant wording in the statement, can get you moving in the right directions so you can uncover some hidden premises that perhaps the person to whom you are speaking perhaps was unaware of. Well, in the case mentioned above, we perhaps know better, but not every case is like that.

Example 3—Accepting or Rejecting Premises

If Eve, in response to God's question about giving the apple to Adam, claims that "the serpent made me do it," God is not going to bother arguing with her about whether or not she can stay in the Garden of Eden. He will just kick her out. He chooses not to begin a discussion with her about responsibility, since His premise is that no one, certainly no serpent, could make her do something. Since God's premise is that Eve has free will, He concludes that Eve made the choice and is responsible. Eve's premise is not acceptable, so God, rather than taking the time to teach her how to reason, just kicks her out of the Garden. He could have, of course, gone through a little question-and-answer period with Adam (What do you mean she bid you eat and so you ate of the apple? If Eve jumped in the Nile, would you jump in too?"), but I guess He was too disgusted with both of them. And He probably had other things to do. For the moment, the two of them were a lost cause and they would have to learn from experience. Children!

Unlike God in the *Book of Genesis*, when you have something important to figure out, you have to take time to reason. If this involves speaking to someone else about his/her stance on an issue, you have to take time to uncover that person's reasoning. Sometimes you may sense a premise lies behind a premise, and you might think you know what that is. Hold off on that. <u>Ask, don't assume</u>, if you want to know how someone arrived at a conclusion. You may think there is *a hidden assumption* behind the conclusion. Go ahead and ask.

Example 4—Fathers and Sons: Uncover Hidden Assumptions, Premises

For example, if a father of a sixteen-year-old male says that it is acceptable for his son to drink alcohol, but that his rule is, his son must do it only in the house and only when either mom or dad are around, you must ask him for his premises.

One premise might be factual, i.e., his son drinks outside the home, or so he believes. You might ask him what *caused* him to believe this was and is a fact.

Another premise he might hold is that he can control his son's drinking if he stays around while his son drinks. You should ask him, "Do you think that you can control your son's drinking if you are in the house?" Then ask, "What leads you to believe this?"

Could you ask this father if he drinks? Yes, but you should be aware that <u>this may cause the discussion to go off track</u>. The *question at issue* concerns his son, not him, and your objective is not to place blame, but to get the father to reconsider his position. If you definitely think you must ask this, you should phrase it in an objective way: ask, "Do you drink alcohol?" not "Do you also like getting loaded?" If he says he does drink, then of course you will ask him "Why?" and then ask him if he thinks that his son drinks for the same reason. The first question is foundational to finding out the *causal premises* that will follow. If you find out that he thinks his son drinks for pleasure, perhaps you could get this father to consider that there are other alternatives. Or, maybe he won't consider your questions seriously. Maybe he thinks drinking alcohol doesn't cause harm and is just fun. Is this the *question at issue* here? Then what would you ask? There may be several aspects of an issue. Focusing on one aspect at a time, in a methodical manner, is best.

The Causal Premise: Premises Used in Cause/Effect Reasoning

Premises are not conclusions or judgments, although people often begin a causal discussion this way. A premise is an *assertion* used as support for a conclusion. An assertion is a positive claim of fact or value. When you assert something, you put forward, declare your belief.

Example: Bill O'Flannagan, the talk show host, may declare his position thus:

> How can anyone condone gay marriages? It's preposterous. Not only that, it is unholy. It's also dangerous. Gay marriages will open the door to allow anybody to get married. Five, six people could get married. People could marry dogs, chickens. What's to stop it, once you change the law?

This brings us to our first kind of *causal premise*, based on what you believe might occur. This *hypothetical* kind of premise goes like this: "If x occurs, y will happen" or "If x happens, y might happen." This type of causal premise is usually based on our past experiences and can be effectively used in deductive argument (as in the case, "if a, then b: not a: therefore not b") or inductive argument ("y might happen"). Are hypotheticals useful? Perhaps, but only if you can convince your audience that what you predict is reasonable. Consider that, logically, this is almost always a risky business. Using objective language, unlike the language of Mr. O'Flannagan, can help.

When discussing an issue with reasonable people, an acceptable premise will use clear, objective language as discussed in Chapter Two. The key to avoiding problems in argument is to phrase a causal premise precisely.

A causal premise is recognizable by the use of the following words: "since," "because," "if," "in order to." To avoid hyperbole, use qualifiers ("might," "could").

Here is an example of an argument with a premise underlined:

No News is Good News? By Andrei Popov

> For the past fifty years, the cable news media have become a tool of one or the other political party in America. Is it any wonder that people are turning to the newspapers or the internet to get their news? The internet is much more likely to be politics-free. We know this because we can see who owns this or that website. We can go to the internet and find information that is relatively politics-free. Some of the best sites are PBS.org and World News.net. If we go to the *Wall Street Journal* website or newspaper, we can check out who owns this site or newspaper. The *Wall Street Journal* is owned by a non-politician.
>
> However, Fox and MSNBC, CNBC are all owned by political personages. Hence, their listeners are barraged with skewed "news" on a daily basis. <u>If a political person, meaning a person with a strong political bias, owns the news site or paper, it is likely that the news one will get there will be slanted one way or the other, right or left.</u>

I wanted to figure out what this author's premise was. So, I first had to ask: What is the thesis? I knew I could not know the basis for an argument unless I knew, or thought I knew, what the thesis was. I also understood that I had to distinguish between the thesis (which requires support) and a premise,(which does not need support because it is, as explained before, a "given" the reader either does or does not accept as is.

I proceeded by reading the argument just for the thesis. I found it in the first and second sentences. Then I put it into my own words, just wrote it out so as to take out the rhetorical question and to make sure I really understood it: "People seeking news today are finding it on the internet or in newspapers rather than on cable television news programs because these programs are politically biased due to their being owned by politicians."

After I figured out the main point or thesis, I asked, another question to determine the premise: What sentence in this text is fundamental as a belief the author needs his readers to accept before the thesis will be agreed to? I then found an explicit (stated) premise there in the text, a statement without which the thesis would be untenable, unreasonable:

This idea, "If a political person, meaning a person with a strong political bias, owns the news site or paper, it is likely that the news one will get there will be slanted one way or the other, right or left" must precede the thesis, is necessary to support it. Look over the first couple of paragraphs of the Declaration of Independence in Chapter 7. See any implied causal premises?

The Definition Premise: Making the Meaning Clear

A *definition premise* is a kind of premise that is largely used to provide the speaker's definition of a concept. If a premise lacks clear language, contains vague, mostly abstract words, it may be an unacceptable premise. You should use clear, specific language to make sure you have an acceptable premise. Language is the basis of complex reasoning functions and our communications, of course. There are more wars, marriages, and divorces started because of language than anything else. I don't think any of us spend enough time defining to others what we mean. Language can hurt and language can make our day. Language has power, and in the wrong hands, language has the power to destroy. The Declaration of Independence has many definition premises as do some of our other government documents and many of our statutes.

DISCUSSION 3.1

Read The Declaration of Independence in Chapter Three. Annotate and quote two definition premises. Discuss what is being defined. Do you accept these premises? Explain.

Example 5—What Is Life?

The topic that causes more incivility between two groups these days has got to be abortion. Gay rights is up there, but abortion wins I think when it comes to the murk and mire that can be thrown in to muddy the waters as to the real question at issue. As abstract words pile up, politicians do their best to keep the issue murky. Mr. Bean might say that he believes in "right to life" but then the next day he says he meant the life of the mother and wants to make some exceptions to allow abortion if the life of the mother is at stake. People differ on their definitions of when "life" begins. If we don't ask, the politicians, I bet, won't tell. Mr. Bean could say to a group accusing him of vagueness, "Oh, well, when I think of *life* as in *prolife*, I mean . . ." Now he is clearer, since he has given his definitive premise. We simply MUST ASK FOR DEFINITION.

Some people think that "life" begins at the point of conception. Some people think life means being born, out in the world here with the rest of us. Prolife and prochoice people rarely reach agreement and accept one another's definitions, so they usually leave one another alone. Unfortunately, sometimes the process of defining becomes such a headache for some people that they become violent and buy guns. I think it's better to keep trying to define and *keep an open mind*. <u>Listening to an idea doesn't mean you accept it.</u> Listening and asking questions can't hurt, can it?

DISCUSSION 3.2

Abstract words like "life" or "teenage violence" can cause heated debates. People should first ask one another for their premises and make sure they have clear definitions. Some *definition premise* examples are below. Do you find these premises *acceptable*?

1. Truth is relative.
2. Abstinence is the best form of birth control for teenagers.
3. People who smoke cigarettes are drug addicts.

Notice we don't include should or must statements. Save those words for your thesis, your conclusion.

You should understand that a premise is stated in order to create a solid foundation to build an argument. Be aware that whatever kind of premise you state, whether causal or definitive, your reasonable listener will, more likely than not, want to discuss it with you. ***Don't defend it. Explain it.*** If you truly believe what you have stated in your premise, then perhaps you should try to offer another version of the same idea so that your listener can better understand. Don't presume that your teacher's or your friend's disagreement with your premise is the end of the discussion. Try to revise your wording. Of course, you may just have to agree to disagree, like the "pro-life" and "pro-choice" people. Well, at least you tried and you understand the basis for your disagreement.

Keep in mind that in order to have an acceptable premise you need to avoid absolutes by using *qualifiers*, and never settle on one thing as the only cause. Use clear language in your assertion. Of course, there is no 100 percent foolproof method to articulate an acceptable premise, since the meaning of what you are saying will always depend on your audience.

DISCUSSION 3.3

Discuss these 4 questions. First, read this quote, taken from Truthdig.com:

> "In the disasters at the Massey coal mine in West Virginia and on the BP oil rig in the Gulf of Mexico, people were killed. So why aren't the executives of these companies behind bars?"

1. Is this a factual, neutral, acceptable premise ? Is there a causal premise?

2. Does the above communicate a fact or assume something not in evidence?

3. What do you think of the wording? Do any words affect your decision to accept one of the premises stated or implied in the above quote?

4. Would qualifiers help? How?

EXERCISES 3A–D FOR CHAPTER THREE

EXERCISE 3A

Read the Declaration of Independence in Ch 7 of *Making Sense*. Annotate, looking for premises.

What is the thesis of the document? (We logically have to find the thesis before we can uncover the premises upon which the thesis is based, so find that first and write it in your own words here:

_____

_____

In your own words, write three causal premises that are stated in the Declaration of Independence.

1. _____

2. _____

3. _____

EXERCISE 3B

Read the essay by Carl Rogers

A. In Chapter 7, you will find the essay on communication by Carl Rogers. What is the thesis of this piece? Write it in your own words, 2 sentences max, beginning with the word "Communication." Do not write what he believes or thinks. Write the thesis of that article only. No research on Rogers. Your own ideas only.

Communication. . . .

_____

_____

_____

B. Write 2 premises Rogers holds, again, in your own words and based solely on the article in Chapter 7 of this text. Be careful: don't write a conclusion (see Ch 3)

1. _____

2. _____

EXERCISE 3C

Read the "Allegory of the Cave" in Chapter 7. <u>Do not use any researched information to answer the three questions below. Your own words, please.</u>

1. What duty must Glaucon perform if he wants to be a philosopher? Why? What is the implicit premise regarding the duty of a philosopher?

_____

_____

_____

_____

_____

2. How does "Allegory" relate to what we have been studying?

_____

_____

_____

_____

_____

3. What is one of Socrates' definition or causal premises regarding politicians?

_____

_____

EXERCISE 3D

Go to Chapter 7 and locate the story "Massaab." First, figure out her thesis: What conclusion does the main character come to and what decision does she make? Then, write below two premises the author must hold in order for her to retaliate. Explain your answers for each, based on your understanding of the lessons you have studied so far in Making Sense.

Employ quotes as necessary to explain your reasoning.

_____

_____

_____

_____

_____

_____

CHAPTER FOUR

Definition

denotation	illustration
connotation	opposition
negation	synonym
stipulation	quotation

Denotative Definition (The literal, objective definition of a word)

There are several ways to go about *defining abstract ideas*. One approach is to use *denotation*, or dictionary definition. This is the most objective way to define. You can get denotation from a reference book, an encyclopedia, or a textbook. A medical doctor may define the word "addiction" in certain terms, but when you go to a psychology text, you may find a different answer. They are both denotative definitions, but they are used in different ways to explain different phenomena.

The English language is complex. Even the literal definition of *concrete* words can change. Depending on whether you're standing on British or American soil, the definition of the word "banger" could be "sausage" or "gang member." This is why George Bernard Shaw, the author of *Pygmalion* (which later became *My Fair Lady*), described America and England as "two countries separated by a common language."

Still, denotative definitions have the effect of sounding objective, more factual, and so they are the most likely to be understood and the least likely to provoke an emotional response. They are thus the most likely to be accepted. When you cite the most common, literal definition in the dictionary, or give a *denotative definition*, you *solidify* your meaning. Of course, this depends upon the dictionary you are using and on the definition from the dictionary you choose. The word "mother" is defined as "one who gives birth or raises a child." We can all settle on that as the meaning we usually associate with that word.

Do we need to define denotatively all the time to make our premises acceptable? Of course not. We're not walking dictionaries. We need to use objective definitions when we anticipate some objection to the use of some word. That will depend on our audience. We can assume that the word "mother" will not be construed to mean "a gummy, slimy substance found in bacteria in vinegar" unless we are in some sort of scientific type of discussion. (See #3 or #4 definition of "mother" in your dictionary.)

Connotative Definition (Personal, subjective connections we make between words)

In the sentence, "Working parents neglect their kids," we have perhaps another reason to start a heated discussion. The trigger word, "neglect," is combustible. It will cause some people to pop off, "That's not true!" You've pushed their buttons. The word "neglect" is said to have a *negative connotation.*

Likewise, words can have *positive connotations.* Whether or not a word or phrase has a positive or negative connotation depends upon the *context,* or surrounding words; the listeners, viewers or readers; and the particular situation. When we use a connotative definition, we are not trying for the truth, but rather trying to express our opinions, or show the opinions of someone else.

Connotative definitions are those that connote meaning. "Con" in this case means "with." So the verb "to connote" means "with notes." The *notes* words come *with* are mental notes, associations you may attach to words like "motherhood." For example, most of us have different *connotations* with the term "motherhood." My picture of motherhood is not yours.

Connotative language is to some degree subjective, although in some cases, as when you speak connotatively while using a metaphor or a simile, a picture word, you are speaking both objectively and subjectively. We'll discuss this more under "figurative language." But for now, we can think of it this way: When people are giving you their connotations for a word or phrase, they are telling you what words and/or images they normally associate with that word or phrase. Unfortunately, this subjective, personal definition of a word is not always acknowledged as being just a connotation. Some people think their connotative language is denotative, i.e., objective. They will consider you crazy for asking for a definition of a word when "Everybody knows what it means!" They don't realize that their *connotative language* is subjective, expressing opinion as opposed to informing people of some fact.

Often an author may *assume* that you are going to understand and agree with his perspective, his language, and his definition of a word such as "mother." Read the following article to see what I mean with regards to what can happen when an author assumes we accept his definition. Maybe you'll disagree with the author's connotation of the word "mother." See if you can find where the author (let's call him Mr. Popov) defines this word.

Article 1—Abortion of the Nuclear Family

I think everyone knows that there is little help out there for our crumbling family units to continue to exist. We have been let down by our educational systems, our religious leaders, and our own culture. At one time, the mother was the head of a household that functioned like a smooth flowing atom. She was maybe employed outside the home after her children reached school age, working as a nurse or a teacher's aide, but rarely did she enter what traditionally have been held to be men's jobs. Such a woman was the center of her family, someone to respect and someone to go to for advice. She mended her family's socks like she mended their physical and spiritual wounds and thought nothing of it.

These days, a woman who stays home to care for her family is scorned and ridiculed by working women. Is it any wonder that such a woman turns to soap operas, or alcohol, or other women's men? With little to do around the house, thanks to modern appliances, she has time on her hands and is without focus or self-esteem. Naturally, the woman may seek solace in destructive ways.

Of course, there are some females who will use the extra time to take cooking or language courses. I'm not saying that all mothers are beset with frustration and boredom. But many have become accustomed to a lazy lifestyle. Once finished with their few chores, they spend their days watching soap operas and sleazy talk shows that undermine our national family values. No wonder our children are getting the wrong images of family life.

Such a condition naturally fosters bored, listless children. Is it any wonder there are so many gangs today, what with the lack of a respectable role model at home? Children killing children, fourteen-year-olds popping ecstasy, getting pregnant, drinking beer, smoking marijuana.

The abortion of the nuclear family is also a result of our rapacious media. These money-hungry hounds will splash pornography and violence over the Internet, which encourages our children to behave badly.

Our politicians lie and have sex with their hired help. Corporations overcharge us all, while banks offer a mere 2 percent interest on savings accounts. Meanwhile, our schools do not have money to buy updated textbooks or pay for enough competent teachers. They've got my son's football coach teaching world history!

This is a sad time for our country, as the future becomes ever more bleak. What was once a great country is now a country torn apart. Is the Lord punishing us for our excesses, our lust and greed, our blindness to truth? Who can we turn to for moral guidance? There is no one. We need our mothers back. Who else can we turn to for moral guidance if not them? What could possibly be more rewarding for a woman than to nurture and guide the future of America?

Women of America, forget the images you see on television of the successful female lawyers, doctors, or politicians. We need you and we loved you the way you were. Bring the concept of a loving, stable mom back into the minds of our youngsters and our young, struggling fathers. You were once the guiding light of our families and can be so again, if only you will put down your paychecks and pick up our country.

—Andrei Popov

DISCUSSION 4.1

1. What is this author's thesis?
2. What is this author's definition of a "mother?" What are a mother's duties? Therein we find his premise.
3. Try to identify three premises and discuss whether or not you accept the premises. Use language analysis and cause-effect analysis to explain.

Stipulative Definitions

When we *stipulate*, we confine, we narrow the possible definitions our audience may associate with our words. In a discussion of parental neglect, reasonable people don't discuss all parents of all kids. We don't even discuss all parents of teenagers. Stipulative definitions narrow or specify a particular meaning:

"Parents who neglect their children, *those who work until 7 p.m. at night, five days a week and don't return home from work until 8 p.m.,* miss out on the lives of their children." This is much less likely to start a heated argument than "Working parents neglect their kids."

Defining by Opposition and Negation

Opposition

Defining by opposition is sometimes useful when we feel at a loss for a definition. Often we use words that seem to defy definition. A dictionary or a thesaurus (a book of synonyms) will just not do. Words like "life," for example, are very hard to define. A critical thinker might start, therefore, by defining what "death" means. In this case, one way we can approach the task of defining is to provide an example of what we see as opposite to our concept of death. One has to be careful when identifying a word as being opposite. "White" is opposite to "black," but "dog" is not the opposite to "cat."

Objective thinkers like to find and discuss gray areas. We see people and events as complex. We value individuality and see each case and appreciate it as separate and unique before fitting it into a category. We usually question the validity of any categorization. Very few things in this world are opposites. People say men and women are opposites, but both are humans and have much more in common. Same for Republicans and Democrats, Whigs and Tories, Christians and Muslims, to math and English majors.

To see real opposition, we have to go to extremes. In vs out. Up vs. down. We must consider: do these two concepts have nothing in common? Sure, in and out, up and down are both directions, but there is no way one can go up and down at the same time (unless on is appearing in a Douglas Adams book!).

Be cautious before ascribing opposition to a pair or group of things, people.

Negation

Like defining by opposition, definition by *negation* attempts to show what a word does not mean. One Japanese man, speaking of his soldierly activities in 1938, in Nan King, China, described the rationale behind his platoon's raping and killing of hundreds of girls and women by saying that he and his platoon thought of them as human when they were raping them, but once they were killing them, they thought of them as *animals.*

You can see that animals are not *human.* It is easier to kill animals, easier on the conscience. Hitler used the same rationale in his autobiography *Mein Kampf.* By referring to certain races as animals, not human, he could at once glorify his own race and segregate, and perhaps even try to destroy (negate), the other. Such analogies are favorites amongst bigots.

This is exemplary of the "they are not like us so they are inferior" kind of mentality that we may have heard in high school. Of course, Hitler's application of the idea went to an extreme. A good example of this kind of extreme's application in America can be seen in the realistic, albeit fictional film *American History X.*

Negating does not have to be used for a negative effect. Negation can help me clarify something to you in a way I might not otherwise be able to. If you refer to me as an alien, I might be able to set you straight by using negation:

"I'm not an *alien.* I'm not a *foreigner.* I'm an *immigrant,* from Mexico, in this country to make a better life for myself."

Synonyms

Synonyms, words that have the same meaning, are not always helpful, and indeed may cause further argument, so choose your synonyms carefully. Denotative synonyms, those that convention dictates are clearly connected to the words they define, are best. Connotative synonyms are more likely to cause confusion. People discussing moral issues often entangle themselves in connotative synonyms, and this causes the conversation to go in circles.

Illustration (Example) Definition

An *illustration* is a way of giving the reader an example of what you mean. When you illustrate, you show a scene, reference a familiar situation using concrete details to make a connection between that situation and the one you are explaining. There are some cases when you need to go into an example of what you mean. These definitions, by their very nature, tend to become subjective as the example is developed. That is because the examples you select and the way you develop the examples are drawn from *your* experiences, your knowledge. When you say, "Let me illustrate what I mean by this," or "Let me show you an example of what I consider a good mother . . ." you are not showing just a "factual account" of some event. The degree of objectivity you wish to obtain is also an issue. You may start out objectively, but may drift into the realm of subjectivity if you start thinking it is necessary to "make your point." This is a misuse of *definition by example.*

We can see how this "misuse" of example to support a viewpoint can get out of hand. Some writers of how-to books do this, when they give us case scenarios that are entertaining to read, but not quite factual and therefore not really useful or practicable. Some social scientists write this way, as in the case of Article 2 below. Like Article 1, which I also wrote under the pseudonym of Andrei Popov, this article is an example of an extreme. Here we see an actual "abuse" of definition by example or *illustration.* Look closely at the subjective, interpretive language in Mr. Popov's next article:

Article 2—The Power of Body Language

Tom and Nancy Smythe are seated at a table in the lounge of Luigi's Italian restaurant. It is 7:30 p.m. and they have been served drinks. They have been seated for half an hour. Tom is actively drinking his gin and tonic. Nancy is staring at the widescreen television. Her drink is full. Tom's lips are covered in salt, and he moves them as he looks at his cocktail napkin. Nancy stares at the Raiders game on the screen.

Tom is showing he needs to talk to someone and is lonely. Nancy is remote and just sitting quietly, politely waiting for the waiter to seat them for dinner.

Across the room sits Carlos. He looks at his watch and then agitatedly shifts his glance from the entrance to the clock. Anita arrives, tosses her head, waves at him. Upon reaching the table, she leans over, grabs his face, and kisses him full on the lips. Seated closely for the next half an hour, they lovingly gaze into each other's eyes and wave their arms as they converse boisterously. Anita smiles and Carlos keeps direct eye contact with her at all times.

Carlos and Anita care deeply for each other. They show it through their body language.

These are just two examples from which we can plainly see that around the globe, different ethnic groups behave with different body language. The English typically do not display affection in public, while those of Latin descent are often seen placing their arms around one another or gesturing to show emotions.

Likewise, men and women have their own ways of communicating through body language. Gender differences are evident when we go into any bar. We see a woman there who is obviously interested in the man across the way. She tilts her head, touches her hair, smiles, flashes her eyes, nods, and may even rub her legs. Her pupils may dilate.

A man, on the other hand, may stroke his hair or chin, wink, or adjust his tie. He may take out his wallet and raise his glass at her. He may place his left hand in clear sight, allowing the woman to see that he wears no wedding band.

Such clear signals are learned from childhood. In a sense, we are all just products of our environment. Thus we have this cultural body language to help us learn the truth about one another, our inherent differences.

—Andrei Popov

You see what I mean by the way examples can be misused? Perhaps there is some difference between British and Latin people, but is this a fair example? What makes it unfair is the use of language, the *slanted* descriptions. The connection between gender and body language, asserting that one can distinguish "male" from "female" body language, is elusive and treacherous. Much is omitted from this short essay.

DISCUSSION 4.2

1. What is this article missing that would make it more reasonable?
2. What slanted language do you see?
3. Which sentence contains an unacceptable definition premise? Is it clearly stated or implied?)

Illustrations can be useful. If I want to explain the word "humanity," I might use the Nazis as a counterexample. But it would be unfair of me to compare democrats or republicans to Nazis, unfair and illogical. We have to watch out for this sort of extreme, generalized thinking and try to help others avoid it. We should think carefully before placing people in groups.

However, sometimes we might want to help young people, especially those we are close to, get a feel for our own set of values. During a discussion with my 5-year-old daughter, I was asked what I meant by "good people." I used my mom and dad as examples. I probably made them look better than they were, but I showed her things that they did (taking care of strangers, old people; letting people get on the freeway instead of trying to crowd them out) out of the goodness of their hearts, doing things or not doing things for no other reason other than they saw it as their duty to consider other human beings and to help as far as their limited means would allow. Helping other people, I explained to her, was a good thing and part of the lives of "good people."

Quotations

"Society everywhere is in conspiracy against the manhood of every one of its members."

—Ralph Waldo Emerson, "Self Reliance," Essays, First Series, 1847

You all know how *quotations* inserted into a discussion or debate can add to the authority of your statement. Now you can see them as just important ways to clarify your meaning. Choose quotes carefully. Don't just rely on slogans. They aren't, usually, real quotes. Many things you might think are quotes are slogans ("Be all that you can be"). When I encourage you to use quotes to clarify your meaning, I am considering that most of you don't know many quotes, let alone the names of the people behind them. I've given you some space to try to recall a significant quote. You know, words to live by.

Who Said It?

Directions: Below is a list of four quotations just for fun. See if you can remember where you heard these. Ask others for help. If you don't know even after investigating, just select the answer that makes the most sense. This is to be done just for fun.

1. "It was the best of times. It was the worst of times."
   a. Charles Darwin
   b. Jesse Jackson
   c. Charles Dickens
   d. Mark Twain

2. "Facts are stupid things"
   a. Ronald Reagan
   b. Ernest Hemingway
   c. George Lukas
   d. Dali Lama

3. . . . life, liberty and the pursuit of happiness.

    a. Abraham Lincoln

    b. Oliver North

    c. Thomas Jefferson

    d. the Beatles

4. "Ask not what your country can do for you. Ask what you can do for your country."

    a. Richard Nixon

    b. R. P. McMurphy

    c. Robert Kennedy

    d. John F. Kennedy

Answers: 1d; 2a; 3c; 4d (Which of this answers surprised you? Why? What were you assuming?)

Other Ways to Define

Metaphor, Similes, Personification, Analogy, and Symbol: Figurative Language

Figurative language is often used to give abstract ideas a "figure" or shape so that you can picture the concept. Though not usually recognized as methods of definition, defining is part of what they do. Thus they can create some sense of objectivity. On the other hand, they definitely carry connotations. The *objectivity* comes with the fact that they reference concrete objects with which we are familiar. Why is a heart a symbol of love? Think about it. With figurative language, the thing referred to is solid and it has some facet in common with the idea being clarified. This is not to say, however, that the effect of figurative language is to substantiate fact. *Figures* create *impressions.* When you make an abstract idea concrete by using some concrete object that people can see, you are just making the idea solid. That doesn't make anything a fact. (If it did, fiction writers would have a lot of explaining to do!)

Still, metaphors, similes, and personifications are very powerful. A picture says a thousand words, especially if the audience is receptive to creative, imaginative language. While you are reading a work by your favorite science fiction writer, you believe the story. Why? Vivid language, picture words cause imagery to be displayed in your mind. A figure in language has this same effect.

Try to think of creating this type of language as a tool for nonfiction rather than fiction. Use it as a device to facilitate truth rather than as a semantic mechanism to persuade or trick. As a critical thinker trying to *reason*, you aren't trying to trick someone or manipulate someone when you consciously choose figures of speech. You are trying to clearly, honestly "represent" your concepts and at the same time engage your audience.

Referring once again to Socrates, you might check out his "Allegory of the Cave," from Book VII of *The Republic*. He allows one of his students to "see" the difference between ignorance and enlightenment by creating an analogy, an extended figurative representation. It is quite instructive, a useful illustration of how figures can make abstract ideas concrete and more credible.

Metaphors are figures of speech that equate one thing with what it is not. They give shape often to abstract concepts. For instance, if my brother says his ex-girlfriend is ugly, I don't know what he means and the message doesn't leave a lasting impression. However, if he says she is a warthog, I get a pretty vivid idea of his opinion.

We use this kind of language every day. Indeed, we overuse some metaphors to the point where they are no longer really effective. Metaphors are only really effective if they accomplish the desired effect. Saying, "This allied effort to reduce nuclear war was only a stopgap" will probably be somewhat understood, but a clear image and definition would probably not occur in the minds of many people.

Metaphors, unlike similes, do not use a comparative term such as "like" or "as" to compare. Instead, metaphors equate one thing with another. In a way, they are stronger, more instantaneous, and yet subtler than similes.

Through working on your metaphoric language, you can refine your language and make it your own. Your words should represent you, and you are unique. Your metaphors should give a clear, unique picture of how *you* see things. At the same time, they should be clear and familiar enough to be objective. "I've got a lead weight in the pit of my stomach, a feeling of deep heaviness," is something most people can picture and still it would say something about you, your frame of reference.

On the other hand, using what George Orwell, in "Politics and the English Language," called "dying metaphors" only *lumps you in* with everybody else saying the same old thing. People tune out to such language. Language, especially metaphors, should bring energy and life into a conversation. Remember, a picture can say a thousand words.

You don't have to go through any complicated process to find metaphors. The objects you use for comparison can be simple animals or shapes. W. B.

Yeats, in the following excerpt from a 1920 poem, mixes concrete and abstract language by using metaphors to draw a picture of the world. See how many metaphors you can find. Are they effective?

Turning and turning in the widening gyre
The falcon cannot hear the falconer;
Things fall apart; the centre cannot hold;
Mere anarchy is loosed upon the world,
The blood-dimmed tide is loosed, and everywhere
The ceremony of innocence is drowned;
The best lack all conviction, while the worst
Are full of passionate intensity

—"The Second Coming" 1920

Effective, powerful metaphors can compare one thing to another so as to give a clear picture and evoke a specific feeling about the object or person being compared. You can create metaphors easily by mentally listing things that exist, concrete objects from nature or technology. Concentrate on some particular aspect of an object, something in your imagination or view. This can be a texture, a color, a speed, curvature, any particular aspect. Try to describe it specifically, using detailed adjectives and vivid verbs. When I say, "I see in your eyes the azure sky of the evening we spent in Las Vegas," I am drawing a metaphor from nature, but the word "azure" is not familiar to everyone. It sounds nice though, doesn't it? When I say, "Rosie's movements, cold and robotic, frightened the Jetson family children," I am using a metaphor from technology. Is this effective? It is if I want the children to be scared. Robot nannies aren't very nice things to imagine.

Similes are not the same as metaphors, but they do compare two things that are seemingly different but share some aspect. Unlike metaphors, similes use a comparative term in between the two things being compared. For example, I don't say that my husband *is* a beast in the morning, but rather say he acts *like* a beast.

Other comparative words that are typically used when creating similes are "as," and "resembles." Similes are created when you use any comparative term: "His words comforted me, *as though* they were each tiny fingers massaging my back and neck, flowing over my tense, contorted, twisted soul."

The same rule for metaphors applies to making similes effective. Stay away from the ones you regularly hear unless they are particularly powerful and appropriate. Remember, you want to speak so that what you say is clear and memorable. Don't say, "The missile belched fire like a Roman candle." What the heck is a Roman candle, and why does it belch? You can do better.

Personification is when you give a human attribute to something that is nonhuman. For example, when I say, "America weeps for her fallen soldiers," I am personifying the abstract concept of America. This is effective because, along with creating a picture for you to hold and recall, it adds sympathetic appeal, humanity, while also making the idea concrete. Again, you should try to be original when personifying and not use overused or outdated images.

DISCUSSION 4.3

1. Is Uncle Sam still effective personification for America?

2. What person or statue of a person would more accurately depict America from your perspective? Why?

3. Who personifies goodness and wisdom for you? Why? Dissect the person's attributes and explain your premises.

Again, we can see Socrates using concrete language to explain abstract concepts. In the work "Crito," he has the Laws speak to him, question him as to his ethics and principles. This Peroration of the Laws is also known as the personification of the Laws. Such a device humanizes the concept. This work is very interesting because it shows how the Laws, a true rhetorical master, employs various appeals, ethos, logos and pathos, to convince Socrates to stay in jail and take his medicine. The Laws speak to Socrates and tell him that he owes to them everything, his family, his livelihood, everything (pathos appeal, here appeal to guilt; pathos appeal is appeal to emotion). The Laws tell Socrates that if he leaves, his friends and family will suffer disrepute, or worse (more pathos appeal). Quite deftly, the Laws employ logic, or *logos appeal*, and *ethos appeal*, appeal to ethics and ones good reputation, in one fell swoop: What kind of role model will he be for his students if he escapes? That does it. Socrates loses the argument (to himself).

Symbols often represent abstract concepts, but they are only effective if the referent, the thing to which they refer, is familiar and easily recognized by the audience. A band, or any ring on the left hand, on the finger next to my pinkie might symbolize to some people in some cultures that I am married. A cow is a symbol in India, but here in America, it may symbolize only a quick, maybe ninety-nine cent meal, or even Mad Cow disease.

Wag the Dog, a movie made in the late 90s, made fun of symbolism, especially the symbolic power of ribbons. Some people see this ribbon-wearing symbolism as over done and so reject the symbol, while others happily wear their red, yellow, or whatever ribbons to show support.

Some people think their cars are "status" symbols, while others who see them drive by do not think so. So, symbols are symbolic only if the people communicating, or attempting to communicate, agree on their value. Joseph Campbell, Sigmund Freud, Arthur Symonds, Carl Jung, and many others have, for various reasons, discussed symbols and asserted the power of certain symbols. To this day, symbols are being created (or destroyed) to inspire fear and loyalty. Symbols are suggestive and representative of people's deepest emotions. Check out Joseph Campbell's *The Power of Myth* to see how cultures share symbols.

Finally, poetry is known for its use of symbols. If you are interested in this subject, try reading some of the authors I have mentioned above, or some poets who use symbolism, such as Sylvia Plath, Gwendolyn Brooks, John Donne, T. S. Eliot, or Bell Hooks, especially if you are a poet or lyricist.

Analogy

As I see them, analogies are more complicated, extended similes or metaphors. They compare situations or conditions in life rather than just simple, static "things" to "things." When I use an analogy, I am creating a more complicated picture. I'll make an analogy for your understanding.

Using a simile is like using a camera to take two single, still pictures of two simple objects so that you can place the pictures side by side. It is not like an analogy, because the interpretation process is so simple and requires so little thought. It does not require us to make many connections between images. The pictures are unmoving, flat and fixed in time. However, an analogy allows us to make several connections, juxtapose images at various angles. If a simile is a camera, what type of equipment is an analogy?

When you make an analogy, be careful that your analogy compares two situations that share several common elements, even though they are distinct. You don't want to compare situations that are glaringly different. Say for example I am a political conservative and I want to make a case against "tree-hugging liberals." I tell them, "Look. They're just trees. It's okay to cut them down. They'll grow back. It's like corn. We harvest corn, use it. It grows back." This would not be a fair analogy to make because trees, regardless of what kind of tree we are talking about, take much longer to grow back. Also, cutting down certain trees in certain areas under some situations can have a much more serious ecological impact. The two situations should not be compared at all.

EXERCISES 4A–E FOR CHAPTER FOUR

4A. Try to stipulate, narrow the definition of the nouns below. Write a sentence that contains each, showing you understand what it means to stipulate.

Excellent Student _____

U.S. Citizens _____

Lie _____

Marriage _____

4B. Read the text in Chapter Four titled The Power of Body Language. Write a paragraph that uses that piece as support (Begin with a comparison: Just as Mr. Popov, in his article. . . . I too. . . .) as you describe a time when you yourself were thinking something similar and drawing hasty and broad conclusions, generalization about people. Where were you? What stereotypes were you using to draw conclusions about people you were observing? Were you aware at the time that you were stereotyping? What do you think caused you to do that? Were you trying to convince yourself of something, as is our friend, Mr. Popov, and explain some phenomenon you had come up with, a reason for something that you thought you understood? Do you still think your generalization has some merit?

_____

_____

_____

_____

_____

_____

_____

_____

_____

_____

_____

_____

_____

_____

_____

_____

_____

4C. Read the Yeats poem in this chapter. What is a gyre? How does that word relate to some other word in the poem? What does the wording "blood-dimmed tide" remind you of? Why do you think that is?

_____
_____
_____
_____
_____
_____
_____
_____
_____
_____
_____
_____
_____
_____
_____
_____

4D. Who or what do you think is symbolic of (or personifies) America today? Explain your answer. Explain your comparative analysis and make the connection clear

_____
_____
_____
_____
_____
_____
_____
_____
_____
_____
_____
_____
_____
_____

Photo by Mirabelle Jones

Imagine you are the person in the photo. Write a paragraph, using descriptive language containing specific adjectives and vivid verbs as well as some figurative language, explaining where you are, how you arrived there and what you are sensing, drawing on your five senses.

_____

_____

_____

_____

_____

_____

_____

_____

_____

_____

_____

_____

_____

_____

_____

CHAPTER FIVE

How to Avoid Faulty Reasoning About Causes

Everybody's got it all figured out. The boys shot their classmates because their parents neglected them. Ted Bundy raped and killed women because he perused pornography. Why does your English teacher hate you? Well, she's been divorced three times. She obviously hates men, you are a man, and so she hates *you*! Why won't your boss give you a raise? That's right. He's a jerk. Why did that other guy get a raise? Right again. He's a jerk too. This is all very simplistic.

Step One: Watch Out for the Three Traps

Trap 1: Nonsensical Answers to the Question "What Caused . . ."

I ask someone, "Why isn't my mail here?" and the person replies triumphantly, "Oh. Well, it should be." "Well, it isn't. So, why not?" "Well, they are supposed to leave it here for you." "Yes, I know. So, where is it?" "Well, it's not here." "Yes, we have substantiated that, but now, let's move on if we can. Where is it?" "I don't know."

What went wrong with this dialogue? Whose fault was all of this nonsense? Mine. That's right. I asked a causal question when I should have asked for a location: "Where is this letter? Do you know?" That would have saved time.

To avoid the whirlpool of nonsensical causal discussions, figure out first, do you really want to know the cause of some error? Where are you trying to get to in this discussion? What do you want to know?

Sometimes the question *is* a causal one, and there is no way around it.

I go back to the mechanic and ask why the tire they just installed seems to be wobbling, and the guy replies, "It shouldn't." Yes, I agree. "Bad tire, bad tire. Naughty tire to wobble like that! You shouldn't do that. Listen to this mechanic. He knows!" This kind of stuff drives me nuts. How about you?

What do you do when someone avoids your causal inquiry and you need to know the cause? Nothing for it but to ask the question again. Whatever you do, don't get trapped in their nonsense. Just keep asking the same question. If you can't get the answer from that person, ask someone else.

This brings us to the real question at issue: Can we always detect faulty, nonsensical causal reasoning? Do we recognize it in the news? Can we easily see ourselves doing it?

Trap 2: Jumping to Conclusions Before All of the Facts Are In

Another kind of problem we can notice pretty easily is when people assume instead of investigate as much as necessary. Some evening television programs where I live rather encourage this sort of thing. They will show a criminal case and give background information. They know the outcome, the eventual jury decision, but they don't release that until the end. Still, they have us call in and vote before all of the facts are in. People start voting sometimes after only ten minutes. They get us to jump to conclusions. In an almost freespeaking American democracy, where so much responsibility is placed upon the people's shoulders to elect powerful individuals as well as to otherwise reason collectively, jumping to conclusions is negligent and possibly harmful. Reasoning over causes should not be oversimplified. Can you think of any examples where either the national or local news began hypothesizing about the cause of something and then later turned out to be totally wrong?

Trap 3: Getting Caught Up in a Diversion or Getting Off the Track by First Trying to Find "Motivation"

People tend, for example, to believe others intentionally did things that often were just accidents, mistakes, or acts of carelessness. This is harmful because we are laying blame where it does not belong. The problem usually occurs when we do two things: 1) we look for a motive first, and 2) we start seeing a motive where there was none. Here's an example of both at work:

George and Jocelyn are in their bedroom arguing while the children are asleep in the next room. They yell under their breath at each other. "You knew you were supposed to be there. You just hate my family." "Now, George, that's not true. You're saying I intentionally didn't show up for your mother's funeral because I hated her." "That's right. You never liked them. You just wanted to get even. I was so embarrassed!" George runs out of the room and Jocelyn sighs and shrugs. Jocelyn realizes that this is just the tip of the iceberg. Can she *prove* to George what she intended? Can people prove what their intentions are? Maybe, but it is very often not the important *question at issue*.

– 67 –

Is the *question at issue* in this case really what Jocelyn *intended* to do? George is mad because Jocelyn embarrassed him by not being there. Did Jocelyn embarrass him? How could she? She wasn't there. Much of this exists, perhaps, only in George's head. What we are really seeing, if we dig for it, is the shadow of George's *premise*, which is that Jocelyn would do something intentionally to get even with his family. If she has prior to this situation expressed some intention to do his family harm, then this could have led George to see her actions in this light. Also, if Jocelyn has done things in the past to scorn his family and has admitted as much, George's conclusion that she did it intentionally to harm his family is based in reason. If she has never expressed an intention nor done anything spiteful toward his family, then George is being unreasonable, drawing an *illogical* inference. George is showing he does not think very highly of Jocelyn's character. That much is evident. That is the real issue, whether she would do something of this sort.

The significance of the above *illustration* is to make clear the uselessness of looking for intention. This can cause you to get sidetracked. What really matters is the cause and effect that we can figure out. If the effect is pain, and you did something to cause the pain, then you should try to do something to fix it. I know. It's too simple. So, how to stay above it all and take a reasonable approach?

We should all use our voice of reason and let it guide us. We must detach. If we are to reason properly about causes and so obtain the desired insight into the matter, we must hold down our emotional voices and quietly, methodically go through the reasoning process. You know what the voice of reason is, right? Sure you do. It's the same one that wants you to read this book!

Step Two: Begin with Deductive Reasoning

The first step to reasoning about causes, after you have managed to cool your emotions, and avoid the pitfalls above, is to consider just what question you really want answered. Is it, "What killed John F. Kennedy" or "Who killed John F. Kennedy"? Or, is it "What caused John F. Kennedy to die"? It is important to note at this point that how you word your question at issue determines just which answer you get.

Everyone will accept the premise, in the shooting case of John F. Kennedy, that "JFK was assassinated." However, not everyone agrees with the conclusion— that one man's bullets killed him. This will forever be a cause for discussion of one type of causal argument using "deductive" reasoning.

In logical *deductive reasoning*, we work by laying down a *premise* in order to lead our readers or listeners to some conclusion. If we can express a premise clearly, and that premise is acceptable, we can perhaps find a little more specific case or cases to fit into that more general truth. This more specific premise, known as the minor premise, fits under and is included in the major one. The *major premise* supports the minor one, and the major and *minor premise* together lead logically to the conclusion. If one accepts both premises, one must by necessity accept the conclusion. The general idea always comes before the more specific one.

> **Major Premise:** If Kennedy was shot from behind by one man, the exit wounds would all be from the front.
>
> **Minor Premise:** There are only frontal exit wounds evident in these photographs.
>
> **Conclusion:** Kennedy was shot from behind by one man.

This gives you what logicians call a formal deductive *syllogism*, which includes a major premise, a minor premise, and a conclusion.

A causal deductive syllogism can begin with an effect.

> **Major Premise:** Child mortality has risen 37 percent this year in the Bay Area.
>
> **Minor Premise:** Dow Chemicals moved into our area this year.
>
> **Conclusion:** Dow Chemicals has caused the children to die.

You can see that syllogisms, because of their structured nature, sound logical. The one directly above is not logical, however. The proximity in time and location may be a reason for us to be suspicious, but the *syllogism* does not work. It is not valid. Why? The two events are *coincidences* that have not been clearly related. You must show some *correlation* in your *syllogisms*. Working from the effect to the cause is always risky. We always risk the skeptic's charge, "That's not true. You can't prove it!" The skeptic is usually right. This is because we can prove only *probability*, which we will discuss in the section on inductive reasoning. A causal argument using a more investigative approach would be necessary to persuade your audience. Still, some effect premises can work:

> **Major Premise:** Fuel tanks have been known to rupture and cause explosions in airplanes.
>
> **Minor Premise:** Flight 800 exploded.
>
> **Conclusion:** There *might have been* a problem with the fuel tank.

The above syllogism works, but notice the close relationship between the premises. Also, notice the words "might have been," which make this conclusion valid.

The traditional, time-honored example of any deductive, **categorical syllogism** is below.

Major Premise: All men are mortal.
Minor Premise: Socrates is a man.
Conclusion: Socrates is mortal.

This is known as an argument by *inclusion. Socrates is included in the larger category stated in the major premise.*

If you decide to argue based on some universal truth, you may begin deductively, and you may be able to outline your argument in a classic syllogism form. A *categorical syllogism* contains a universal proposition, some assertion about all members of a given class, and a particular proposition, some specific assertion about a specific member of that class. You can "see" how this works in the Euler diagrams that represent the categories below:

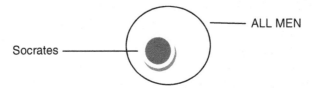

What very large category is missing? If you thought "all mortal beings," then you are correct. Socrates is placed in the category of mortals because it is accepted that he is a mortal and a man. What does it mean to be mortal? You die. Do all men die? Yes. Will Socrates die? He did. He drank hemlock after being found guilty of treason. His mortality and the hemlock caused his death. Below is an illustration of the completed syllogism:

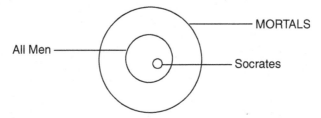

Categorical syllogisms are commonly used to illustrate deductive reasoning that is based on classifications. They illustrate how we categorize people and things and draw conclusions based on this categorization. If done with too little knowledge or thought, the logic breaks down and we get an illogical inference. Sometimes we put people in categories too hastily. We should always try hard to be certain of our categorizations before we commit to them and include someone or something in some general classification.

The above example of categorization consists of "inclusion." We include Socrates in a group, that in turn belongs inside another group. This is a logical category to put Socrates in, but should we put him in a group called "teachers?"

There is another way that we categorically reason, and that is by *exclusion*.

Marsupials, such as kangaroos, carry their young in pouches.
Dogs don't carry their young in pouches.
Dogs are not marsupials.

Naturally, if some dogs are marsupials, then this is invalid. I honestly don't know if there are any marsupial dogs. Do you?

Try illustrating an argument with circles. Here is the major premise:

Teenagers who play Grand Theft Auto are violent. See the three categories?

Draw a circle, call it Teenagers who play GTA.

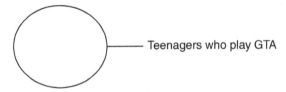

Now let's include a teenager, call him John. John plays GTA. Where does John go? Well, he must go inside the circle titled "Teenagers who play GTA." He fulfills that condition. He is also a teenager, so put him inside there.

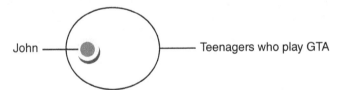

We are still missing one circle. What's missing? We are missing the circle "Teenagers who are violent." Discuss this with others. Where would that circle go? Would John be included in that circle just because he plays GTA?

There are all kinds of people engaged in predicting. For example, some people believe it is effective to engage in an activity we can call "teenager profiling." That's too bad. Teenagers, individual young men and women, are really complicated. They are perhaps the most complicated age group. It's too bad people like to put them in boxes and label them. It's too bad some of them classify themselves using the negative labels they get from their own parents.

The circle exercises above using the Euler diagrams can help us illustrate logical deduction and show problems with categorical thinking. Dogs and marsupials, factual, biological classifications, are a lot easier than classifications of people, especially those that people use to predict human behavior. Deductive reasoning is useful for arguments about universal truths and certainties.

Valid or Invalid Structure? Two Examples

If a categorical syllogism (a nutshell view of a deductive argument) is to be considered logical, it must have *valid structure*. Don't reverse the order of the major and minor premise. Remember: the major premise (claim of fact or value) must be more general than the minor premise.

Here, we see the minor premise precedes the major premise. The syllogism's *structure* is invalid:

> The three journalists I know, two working for the *Herald* and one for the *Review*, said they would be willing to bend the truth in order to publish a hot story.
>
> Journalists are obviously not concerned with the truth.
>
> We should not trust journalists.

This is what happens when we base our opinions, our premises, on personal experiences alone. We invert the specific with the general. This can result in the illogical reasoning, as in the above instance, a fallacy called hasty generalization.

We can make the above journalism argument valid by restructuring and rewording so that the premises are more reasonable (review Chapters One and Three for reasonable vs. unreasonable ways to state opinions). Here we will use a *qualifier* and avoid *hyperbole:*

> Not all journalists are more concerned with reporting the truth than publishing a hot story.
>
> Three journalists I know admit they will bend the truth to beat out their rivals.
>
> We should not trust all journalists.

A *valid* categorical syllogism, or deductive argument that is based on classification, should state the major premise first. The major premise is more general, is the foundation for the minor, more specific premise. (Review Chapter Three before going further if you need to refresh your definition of a *premise.*)

We can look back at the validly structured example that declares Socrates as both a man and a mortal. In that instance, the major (general) premise lays the foundation for the minor (specific) premise.

DISCUSSION 5.1

Are the below SYLLOGISMS valid or invalid, given what you know now from the above lesson in testing for validity?

1. Patricia, Katrina and Allison did not opt to get their children vaccinated.

    Last week at Sequoya Elementary School, ten children came down with measles.

    Parents should be forced to get their children vaccinated for measles.

2. Activities that cause us to divide our focus and awareness of single tasks will reduce our ability to think critically.

    Multi-tasking divides our focus.

    Multi-tasking impairs our ability to think critically.

Inductive Reasoning

After you have stated your major premise, minor premise, and conclusion, not in exact syllogism format of course, you can proceed inductively. We have all seen induction taking place as a detective goes through a crime scene gathering clues. We don't know, at the outset, what the conclusion will be, and we admit this, although we may have a suspicion. Still, we admit that we do not know. The *inductive reasoning* process allows us to find out what probably happened or what probably will happen. It begins with possibility, which again requires us to include and exclude things. We should ask, "What could have possibly caused this?"

"Look for Clues"—Detective Henry Lee

Let's pretend we're forensic scientists, like Dr. Henry Lee, who testified in the O.J. Simpson trial. We enter a room. There is a knife covered with blood by the door. The bloody body of a dead woman is lying on the floor. We begin with a premise: "She was killed with the knife." We just assume this. We then proceed inductively to figure out how she was killed with the knife. There are many factors to be considered, so we must proceed to admit *possibilities before probabilities.*

After the initial, general premise statement, we are left with the familiar murder mystery question at issue, "Who dunnit?" We thus must begin our analysis, our mental operation, *inductively,* and the whole discussion takes on a more investigative, Sherlock Holmes–like tone. This is where we process *knowns* and *unknowns.* When we apply a logical inductive argument, we do not stray far from the initial fact or value that we should all accept as being "true." If we began with the idea that "she was killed with a knife," we have to somehow stay connected to that idea. We will be bringing in specifics, making unknowns into "knowables," or even "knowns," eliminating some knowns in order to present a whole picture. We should come to some conclusion as to who dunnit (with the knife) eventually. How do you convince someone that something occurred for the reasons you think it did? You can think of this type of causal argument, which begins after some deduction and proceeds inductively, by constructing an analogy with me.

The Puzzle Analogy: Constructing the Causal Argument

You (the person reasoning) are briefly showing someone the cover picture on a puzzle box to get him/her interested in recreating the picture with you. You have already worked through the puzzle and know all its parts and where they go. You know these parts well, realize how they relate. You know they are all significant to the whole picture, some more so than others. Most of all, you know that you have all the pieces and that if you connect them gradually, they will make that picture on the box. There is a lot of "what if-ing" that goes on between the two of you as you proceed along the way, a great deal of supposing, and perhaps some errors that need adjusting, but you work it through to the end together.

Those "what if's" are called hypothetical premises. If x then y. If x is present, we get y. If x does not fulfill the condition, we don't get y. While you are trying to explain your causal reasoning to another person, you will have to remember, he/she has not seen the whole picture. You have. Remember, you already know many of the problems that will arise and know the process of connecting the pieces because you have done it before and you can remember almost all of the important steps you took and the errors you made, which you can now help your partner avoid.

The procedure of arguing using deduction and induction is like this. You show someone the box, and then set the cover aside, but not too far away. You begin *reconstructing the puzzle* together. Sometimes you refer back to the whole picture (the premise) to stay on track. You do not lead the other person, but assist, saying, "Where could this one go? Well, it looks like these others, but is it really?" Of course, you know better than to try to force a piece where it does not belong.

Contributing Factors, Necessary and Sufficient Conditions

In the above analogy, the pieces are all simply *contributing factors*, things that have contributed to the ultimate effect. Some pieces are more relevant than others. Some pieces are more concrete, or more important for us to have in order to connect the others. Without these pieces, we could not have a clear picture. Such pieces are "sufficient conditions." The knife was in part sufficient as a factor in the slaying of our hypothetical victim. Other pieces are also more vital, even necessary. Without these *necessary conditions, we have no murder at all. No knife, no murder.* Someone must have done the killing, and there must have been an available victim. More *necessary conditions.* There also had to be a sufficient opportunity for the slaying to take place.

If we proceed to collect evidence that Mr. X did it with the knife, we must somehow prove that Mr. X could have been in that place at that time. He had to have had the opportunity and the means. He has to fit into the scene. If he doesn't, I don't try to force him into the picture. If I'm a prosecutor and I do this, then I have lost my credibility and my integrity. In the Columbine shooting case, there were kids and loaded guns in school together. These were *necessary conditions* for the effect. Take any one of these conditions away and you have no "school shooting."

Remember that if we start out saying, as they do in a court of law, that "that the victim was killed with a knife, and Mr. X's fingerprints were on that knife, and we can prove he did it," then we begin deductively. The fact—the victim was killed with a knife—is a given, an accepted premise. We will then proceed inductively, supposing this and that, making it clear that Mr. X's fingerprints are on the knife, getting witnesses to testify that they had seen him hurt the woman before, etc. We will submit some actual and some circumstantial evidence and perhaps end with a hypothetical. We will build up to the *probability* of Mr. X's guilt. Possibly Mr. X's attorney will do everything in his power to exclude Mr. X as a possible suspect. He will say, "Mr. X, my wonderful client, had no opportunity to kill her. He was working at the knife factory all day!" The comforting aspect of this kind of reasoning is that you can retrace your steps and bring your reader along while you do so.

A Final Suggestion Before You Proceed to Argue Cause: Question What "Sounds Right"

A causal argument concerning people is almost impossible to prove with certainty because of the complexities and variables involved in accurately reconstructing the past. That's why they have us jurors decide "beyond a reasonable doubt." Most of the time, going through a process of reconstructing the past will leave us with some unknowns, but that is okay, because there is a "preponderance of evidence," a vast amount of relevant, factual information, before us. At least, that is what the prosecution hopes we will consider.

We should question first, second, and third assessments of each situation. We should question our own conditioning, what our friends, relatives, and the media have led us to believe are "facts." We need to be honest about our biases from the outset.

How to Avoid Hasty Conclusions

This is one of the best things about critical thinking: You get to listen to yourself think and analyze yourself. In doing so, you come to know yourself better. I'm not saying you'll like what you get to know, but you may avoid some nasty surprises later on.

Be realistic: You do have biases and probably some kind of prejudice against some group. This is not the time to psychoanalyze why. This is the time to "see" and admit that those biases are there. Once you do that in any case where it is appropriate, you can try to lay the bias aside. Listen to your voice of reason. You are, after all, seeking the truth, not trying to win some case in a court room.

As you process ideas regarding causes or effects, be sure to separate the fact words from the value words, or you'll end up with one of those headaches I have mentioned. After coming up with several ways to look at the situation, the *reasonable possibilities,* do a *process of elimination* in order to find a probable cause for the crime. Again, this takes a little more time. What did all of the school shootings have in common? Weapons and kids in school were two important primary factors. What else could possibly have been a *contributing factor?*

Inductive reasoning, working from possibility to determine probability, takes time, but you can't reason logically about causes without this process of including possible causes, then eliminating those that are unlikely or least likely, least important, or least relevant.

Your basic premise of your inductive process should be that there is more than one cause. To proceed, start to assess the credibility of all possible, relevant causes. Question their factual bases. The first step in this process of determining reasonable cause is to substantiate your fact base.

Just the Facts, Ma'am

Ask yourself what relevant facts could have contributed to this particular outcome. Be sure to distinguish fact from opinions. Start with the outcome, and then backtrack. Ask yourself what you don't know. Is any relevant information possibly lacking? Don't assume something was there. Just acknowledge you don't know, if you really don't.

In the Columbine High School shooting/bombing case, for example, not all the facts were known, but this didn't stop the news from reporting things right away. I heard that twenty-three people were killed. I heard people conjecturing as to what caused the shooters to take up arms. They showed people theorizing, with Marilyn Manson music videos and pictures from the game Doom in the background. They blamed violent video games, citing *studies* that showed a definite correlation between game playing and violent behavior. One analyst referred to Harris and Klebold as the *gay trench coat killers.* Was that relevant? I was confused. What were the sufficient conditions to cause this? *Sufficient conditions* are those that, when present, are sufficient to cause some specific effect. The first thing that I thought might be relevant to determine was, "Were they high?" I wondered if autopsies would be done. I questioned their sobriety; it seemed like such a nutty thing to do. (Of course, whether or not they were *gay* would be much more relevant. How silly of me!) It was so frustrating. The attitude of these media people seemed to be, "Let's label the reported criminals, package them, and sell the hypothetical cause. The people want an explanation. Let's give them one." They should have started here: What did the boys need in order to shoot their class mates? Trench coats? Marilyn Manson tapes? Gay tendencies or . . . guns maybe? Yes, guns. Guns in the school. This was a necessary condition without which no school shooting would have taken place.

It's important to question what you think about news stories. You may come away thinking that something was a fact when indeed it was not. It's also very important to stay clear of really irrelevant details and hypotheticals, which media people like to include, possibly for sensationalism. As we watch our televisions or read articles, we should stay away from simply looking for like elements or circumstances. Studies based on this process of comparison and contrast require time and stringent controls. Scientists and serious sociologists use highly regulated methodology before they say that people who do X will also do Y. Many factors could have been similar in the lives of all school shooters. They may have all eaten Cheerios the morning of the shootings and every day for a week previous to the shootings. Did Cheerios cause the outcome? Probably not. We know this is just a coincidence. However, if research scientists study two hundred cases of school shootings and find that 80 percent of the shooters ate Cheerios, the probability of Cheerios being a *contributing factor* would perhaps be taken a little more seriously. Still, we should be careful before doing magical comparative studies. Let's examine one of these.

Let's say we're trying to solve the question "Why do teenagers shoot other kids in school?" Look at the table below. We want to help these guys out, right? So let's conduct an amateur long study. Over a period of six months, we examine the cases of one hundred teenaged school shooters from all over, Nashville, Dallas, Salem, Chicago, and New York. Let's break them up into groups of forty, mixing up the regions just for some objectivity. (Of course this is all subjective!)

Group A	Group B	Group C	Group D	Group E
tvy	twz	tuz	tvw	wyz

Let's say a letter under the column represents spending more than two hours per day on a given activity: t = watching violent television; u = playing *shooting* video games; v = talking on the phone; w = playing contact sports; x = chatting online; y = having a recent argument with a girlfriend; and z = perusing pornography. Now that we have seven *possible contributing factors,* which one of them shows up most often? Is this the reason that teenagers shoot their classmates? Of course not. Obviously such a study would be absurd, but I've seen some similar *studies.* What you should do in almost every case is question the study. Use the list of questions below to evaluate the legitimacy of any study proffered for your acceptance as being legitimately indicative of some tendency inherent in a group of people.

1. Who did the study?
2. Who commissioned the study? Who asked that the study be conducted?
3. When was the study conducted, and over how long a period of time?
4. Who were the people in the study? What was the exact composition of the control group?
5. What controls were used? This means, were they all tested under similar conditions? How was the study conducted?

There are more questions you could ask, but these should be enough to qualify any study as being either on the side of objectivity or on the side of subjectivity. We want our studies to be as cohesive and legitimate as possible before we give them any credence and use them to draw conclusions about cause/effect. If we can't answer at least a couple of these questions, we should not call it a *valid study*. Currently, the issues of hate crimes and racial profiling are being hotly debated in Congress. Our representatives are looking into many studies by universities and think tanks. I hope that the studies they are using are legitimate, don't you?

After you find your possible contributing factors during your research into a cause of some effect, you should ask which conditions that preceded the event, as you know them, were *sufficient* to have caused the outcome. Do all kids with access to guns bring them to school? Is giving kids guns a *sufficient condition* to cause the outcome of a school shooting? No. But, if you have a school shooting, the necessary conditions are guns in a school with people in it.

DISCUSSION 5.2

Try answering these questions during discussion:

1. Iced tea consists of which necessary conditions? Circle them.

   a. ice b. tea c. sugar d. lemon

   If you circled sugar and lemon, then you are not quite understanding yet what is meant by "necessary." Only ice and tea (a and b) are necessary in order to have ice tea . . . okay you do need a container of some sort too. Remember: necessary means "can't be a certain way without it."

2. Go to the findlaw.com website and find the definition for "rape." Which of the below would be necessary conditions for a rape?

   a. sexual intercourse b. unknown assailant c. a female
   d. physical force e. lack of consent

Sometimes people envision a crime, whose name is an abstract word (most names for crimes are abstract words) in a certain way. They picture a scene, get an image and think, "Everyone else sees this the same way I do. We all know rape when we see it." This is not a problem unless these people refuse to see other people's perspectives and analyze and understand the meanings of the words that describe the law. Like a lot of laws, the *crime* of rape does not have a consistent definition. State laws redefine what a rape is and attach various punishments to the crime. And, like a lot of laws, when we look them up, the abstract word for the name of the law is defined by, you guessed it, a bunch of other abstract words. Hence we have lots and lots of busy lawyers.

I hope you understand now what makes for contributing factors, sufficient conditions and necessary conditions.

One of the biggest puzzles for me is global warming. I am pretty convinced the planet is warming. I believe that global warming (now called climate change) is caused by several factors, according to the Intergovernmental Panel on Climate Change (IPCC). More than 2000 scientists, meteorologists, climatologists, marine bio-geochemists, oceanographers and others around the globe have been sharing information, measurements and data about rainfall, ocean temperatures, glacial ice melt and submitting it to the IPCC which has so far filed four reports, reports used by the UN for the Kyoto and the Copenhagen summits. What are the contributing factors to global warming? They believe aerosols, carbon dioxide, methane are a few. How much climate change in the air, land and oceans are we talking about over how much time? What factors could be causing that amount of "change" in that amount of time? (carbon dioxide? methane? global dimming?). Looking at the question at issue—which is "What is causing the amount of change in average temperatures or extreme changes in precipitation amounts, in the last thirty years?"— global scientists have been able to ascertain—with some experimenting—that certain factors are sufficient to cause variations in the climate like the ones they have observed. Sharing and comparing their data, climate scientists are still working on measurements, and they will probably (hopefully) continue to do so, but they have reached some consensus about the causes, the likely impacts of unfettered global warming. If you read their physical report (Working Group #1) you can see what "necessary condition" they all agree on, what they believe is definitely a factor that needed to be in place in order for such rapid increase in global temperatures and other symptoms of climate change to have occurred over the last thirty years. Some people say this is all a bunch of baloney. Well, I say to them, we can figure that out. Read the report first. Then, the baloney detection kit tools set down by Carl Sagan in his book, *The Demon-Haunted World*:

The following are suggested as tools for testing arguments and detecting fallacious or fraudulent arguments:

- Wherever possible there must be independent confirmation of the facts
- Encourage substantive debate on the evidence by knowledgeable proponents of all points of view.
- Arguments from authority carry little weight (in science there are no "authorities").
- Spin more than one hypothesis—don't simply run with the first idea that caught your fancy.

- Try not to get overly attached to a hypothesis just because it's yours.
- Quantify, wherever possible.
- If there is a chain of argument every link in the chain must work.
- "Occam's razor"—if there are two hypothesis that explain the data equally well choose the simpler.
- Ask whether the hypothesis can, at least in principle, be falsified (shown to be false by some unambiguous test). In other words, is it testable? Can others duplicate the experiment and get the same result?

CHAPTER SIX

Fallacies Caused by Faulty Definition and Faulty Cause/Effect Reasoning

I have found it useful to divide fallacies into two types: those caused by lack of clear definition and those resulting from a lack of logical, causal reasoning. There may be more, but I don't see how. These two classes may and do cross over, though. There is some "overlap."

Before going any further, let's be sure to get a clear definition of what a fallacy is in general.

Fallacy: from *fallere* in Latin, which means "to deceive." A fallacy is misleading, leads away from understanding, away from truth. It may be committed either intentionally, as when a politician claims his opponent is an "ugly American," or unintentionally, due to lack of reasoning or thoughtfulness. It may come in the form of an assertion, some sort of declaration or statement; it may be imbedded in a question, known as an interrogative; it may come in the form of a command, known as an imperative; or in the form of an exclamation of emotion. Fallacies are persuasive, so they are not very obvious mistakes in logic. The statement "pigs can fly" is not a fallacious statement because it is absurd.

It is important to keep in mind the Latin meaning and the idea that a fallacy is committed when one makes a serious attempt to be reasonable. Fallacies sound persuasive, but they should not persuade you. They are deceptively persuasive. They do not make sense, yet they're not nonsense.

Important to note is that not all mistakes are fallacies. If a witness genuinely believes she saw the defendant leave his apartment with a real gun, after she has just heard what she believes to be a gunshot, she cannot be considered to have used fallacious reasoning when it later turns out the defendant actually was carrying a water pistol, and the gunshot sound was a car backfiring. Her reasoning was not faulty. She did think she saw a gun, and it was a gun. Her thinking about the "evidence" wasn't all that bad. Maybe her eyesight was.

Maybe she was just too far away. A good lawyer would ask her to stipulate, ask what kind of gun she saw.

List of Common Fallacies (After you study these, you can take the Practice Quiz)

Fallacious reasoning occurs from oversimplification. Look at the list of fallacies below and see if you can see all of these as cases of oversimplifying. Notice, in the quoted material, any lack of clear definition or oversimplified, hasty causal reasoning.

Ad hominem   Instead of addressing the issue, you attack the opponent's character. This usually entails some kind of disparaging remark.

"Mr. Popov is a con artist."

"Howard is a sexist druggie."

When you directly attack a person's character and that attack is personal and irrelevant, you commit an ad hominem fallacy.

• Tu quo que   **A kind of ad hominem** attack that is less direct. Here the speaker counters an attack on his/her own behavior by claiming the other person does the same thing: "Why shouldn't I drink alcohol? You do." You can see how this avoids the question at issue.

Appeal to fear   Instead of addressing the question at issue, you make an emotional appeal to fear. You try to scare the person in order to persuade him or her.

"Do you see this little girl? She will die if she doesn't get help soon."

Some people found the Bush administration to be guilty of this after 9/11, posting their yellow or orange levels every couple of weeks.

Appeal to guilt   Here again, you have an emotional appeal. "*You* have a good life, there in your comfortable living room. *You* have enough to eat. You have enough to spare. Call and help the children."

What they are implying is, "You should feel ashamed. Call us and ease your conscience." Ask, "Is this my responsibility?"

Appeal to pity	"Look at her. She's dying of starvation. Please help."

Not good for an argument because no factual basis is given. During elections, much talk circulates through the debates about the poor seniors. This fallacy is sometimes referred to as *ad misericordium*.

Bandwagoning	"Millions of good, caring people have already donated. Won't you join us?"

"You should just stay quiet or everybody will look at you." You reply, "Okay."

You go along with the crowd for no better reason than to fit in, conform. There should be another reason to "join." If there isn't, it's *bandwagoning*.

Begging the question	Can be a statement, a question, or an answer.

The question being begged is that posed by the person's explanation or question. The person speaking *assumes some fact not in evidence*. There can be a leading question, also called a *loaded question:* Here there is a stated question, and there is an assumption made. A question phrased this way assumes a fact not in evidence:

Loaded Question

"You don't want to buy products that require the torture of little animals, do you?"

Sometimes, there is seeming evasion, where the listener is led around in circles. This particular kind of question begging is called *circular reasoning*. Here especially, the question that is asked is just "begging" to be asked again.

Circular Reasoning

"Why did you drink and drive?"

"I had to get home."

Another kind of question begging occurs when someone avoids an answer to the problem by labeling someone or something. This is called an *epithet*.

Epithet

"Why don't I like Bolenciewicz? He's a jock!"

In the case of the answer given above, the person has just opened up more questions: "What's wrong with jocks?" One might also ask, "What do you mean by 'jock'?" This is a typical case of a fallacy that occurs from lack of definition.

People avoid the real *question at issue* when they question beg. They may play word games. Wordgame players and critical thinkers are often at odds. Wordgame players tend to see words as game pieces. Reasonable, logical people look at words for their substance and meaning. Wordgame players want to win. We should use words for their potential to embody and elicit reason and perhaps truth if our goal is to achieve mutual understanding.

Breaking Down Begging the Question for Further Clarification

With a loaded question, a question is begging to be asked. The speaker has implied evidence that isn't agreed upon when she says, "You don't want to buy products that require the torture of little animals, do you?" The question implies that animals are being tortured. Has this premise been agreed upon? If not, then you have begging the question. The classic example of this type of question begging is evident in the following question to the accused on the stand: "So, when did you stop beating your wife?" Another example is, "You guys know how bad it is to smoke cigarettes, right?" Think back, at this point, on any of the articles you have read in this book. Did any of them show question begging at work? Go through your workday, or listen to people in line at the supermarket. Any loaded questions? I don't even have to tell you to prepare to listen for these during election speeches.

With circular reasoning, your partner doesn't answer but leads you around in circles, right back to your original question. He's got you chasing your own tail. Not much you can do but keep asking the question, maybe in a clearer way so as to limit his ability to do this. If someone asks, "Why do you like Ford better than Honda?" and you reply, "Because Ford is the best!" then you are committing circular reasoning, and the person must again ask you the same question. Circular reasoning is a waste of time.

An *epithet* is a label. Earlier, labeling Bolenciewicz a jock, we are sidestepping the question at issue. This is an impersonal label. It doesn't answer the question about the person Bolenciewicz. Oversimplifications run rampant like free apes in our jungle of fallacies.

Equivocation	This means to give equal voice or value to a word or phrase even though it means different things in different contexts. If I say that "guns" killed people during the school shootings in Oregon and Colorado, and I propose handgun legislation to help stop such shootings, I am equivocating. The "guns" in those incidents weren't handguns.
	Another example: Hey, I have a *theory* as to how humans evolved. My *theory* is just as good as Darwin's.
False analogy	A false analogy occurs for mainly two main reasons, either of which is sufficient:
	1) There are too many dissimilar characteristics, or
	2) The two situations or conditions being compared are too incomparable. For example, you wouldn't want to say,
	"High school baseball players shouldn't have to do homework.
	Pro baseball players don't have to do homework."
	A false analogy is sometimes persuasive. Sometimes it is more obviously false:
	"That girl, Babs, the one in the swimsuit who was raped last night, got what she deserved. She walked by the fraternity at nine o'clock at night. She was wearing nothing but a bikini. Hell, it was like putting chum out for sharks. What's a guy to do? It's human nature. She's got nothing to cry about. You can't control this kind of thing. If I fall asleep drunk on the couch, leave my door open, and a thief comes in and steals my stereo, I deserve what I get!"
	Look at the two tests for a false analogy I have given you (above). What is wrong with this reasoning? Should Babs be compared to a fish? Is she similar to a stereo? Are the things "lost" the same?
False dilemma (either/or fallacy)	"You can't get anywhere in life if you don't go to college." "America. Love it or leave it!"
	I suppose you have heard at least one of these and found at least one to be persuasive. Don't be fooled.

What's wrong? You're only give x number of choices when there are more.

Guilt or glory by association

No merit or blame should be given based only on the fact of people's association with others. Guilt and glory by association attempt to bias us against or for someone based solely on their connection to someone or something.

"Rachel's father was a friend of Hitler's." (Guilt)

"He worked under President Nixon as an aide."(Guilt or glory, depending on your audience)

"She once worked for Mother Theresa." (Glory)

"Oh, don't vote for him. He went to Yale!" (Guilt? Glory?)

Poisoning the well

"This guy has smoked marijuana. He has lied to you for the last twelve years. Look at what he said about the Internet!"

"Well, this guy's an admitted alcoholic. He is an oil-man and wants to help the rich. We can't elect him mayor!"

Poisoning the well is self-explanatory once you under-stand that the "well" is a metaphor for people's minds. The well is the audience; we used to refer to people who sat below the stage as the audience below a stage in a theatre (dramatic not film). This audience is necessary in order for poisoning the well to take place. It's pretty standard fare these days in the world of politics. This causes prejudice. Labels help poison wells (the minds of the audience).

Post hoc, ergo propter hoc

"Why did these kids bomb the school? Well, what happened before then? Ah. They were playing a video game, so that caused them to act violently."

"Post hoc, ergo propter hoc" denotatively means "after this, therefore because of this." When you link an effect to a cause just because the effect happened in proximate time, after some event, then you have post hoc, perhaps. **B occurred after A; therefore A caused B.**

This is how some superstitions work. You may see yourself as having failed an exam because you didn't remember to wear your lucky sweater.

It is important to note: Not every connection to the past, not every stated causal relationship between a previous event and a current one, is a post hoc. Sometimes a statement as to how the past affected the present is a reasonable, logical one.

Post hoc, as you may call it for short, is the most common fallacy I see around me. People jump to conclusions about relationships between events just by virtue of some time connection. This is the problem with this fallacy. These post hoc statements sound reasonable, but they usually contain some overstatement and oversimplify the case. People don't consider long enough before they make the statement "A caused B because A came first."

People should not just look for one cause because there are often multiple causes, a consideration that is painful to some people who have agendas and would like to blame kids' violence on "lack of family values," "lack of moral upbringing," "no prayers allowed in school," or "media violence," which would greatly oversimplify the situation.

Now, let's consider: Would it be post hoc fallacy if we said, "The guns and bombs were significant causes of the killings?" Why or why not?

Slippery slope

Slippery slope fallacy occurs when people make predictions about future events that in all probability will not occur. The formula is **"if x happens, y will occur."** One way to tell you might have slippery slope fallacy before you is if you see/hear the word "will." "If you get a master's degree, you will be rich!"

This fallacy can be avoided if you use the qualifiers "might" or "perhaps".

Many advertisers proclaim that their product "can" reduce fat or anxiety, etc. They are not guilty of slippery slope fallacy unless their product absolutely cannot do what they claim. Another word to use to avoid this fallacy is "usually." You want to stay away from claims like, "It will work for you ninety-nine times out of one hundred!"

Finally, if the prediction is indeed a *probability*, then it is not slippery slope. If I say the following, I am not guilty of slippery slope:

"If John goes out and drinks half a quart of gin to-night and tries to drive home, he's probably going to have an accident."

A Final Word on Fallacies

There are many more specific fallacies. There may be more than one fallacy in a given statement. At this point just be aware of the need to avoid vague wording and simplistic cause effect. Studying every kind of fallacy so that you have a name to put on someone's defective reasoning is not the way to achieve better understanding. The way to do that is to practice listening carefully for premises and questioning what seems unclear. So, we're right back where we started. Go ahead and practice what you have learned.

Fallacies Practice

Practice your understanding of fallacies. Write in the name of the fallacy or fallacies you see here. Yes, there may be more than one. Some possible correct answers follow.

1. The people at the Your Choice clinic promised me I would have a girl if I ate cheese while I was pregnant. I ate cheese for five months while I was pregnant. Guess what? I had a girl!

2. If you don't stop teenagers from playing violent video games, pretty soon you're going to have school shootings in your own neighborhood.

3. Either you vote for Gore or you vote for one of the Republicans who will guarantee you end up paying more taxes for military spending.

4. We all want the best cars, the best computers, and the best healthcare. Why shouldn't we try to genetically engineer the best babies?

5. We need to learn more history so we can avoid painful experiences. A baby learns not to put its finger in the fire. If we learn about the painful experiences in history, then we will not repeat them.

6. Wife to husband: "Why did you hang up the phone when I came in? What don't you want me to hear?"

7. We all know that teenagers are the cause of most car accidents. The legal driving age should be raised to twenty.

8. You're a coward. You have no guts. You can't even face me. Why are you avoiding my eyes?

9. Chief of police: "I am sure that this is going to cause the community to cry out in horror. Such a situation is hard to explain. Such a light sentence for an obviously guilty drug pusher will create community outrage."

10. Kids shouldn't have guns in school. The Columbine incident was a disaster. We need tougher handgun laws. We should also have trigger locks.

11. If this evilutionist is allowed to teach this godless science, our land will become like Sodom and Gomorrah, and the young will turn upon the old.—*Inherit the Wind*

As you will see below, there may be more than one fallacy at work. Look back to the relevant chapter pages to see if you can figure out why the answer is different from what you thought.

Answers to Fallacy Practice

1. Post hoc (she had a girl because she previously ate cheese).

2. Slippery slope/begging the question (it probably won't happen that they will start shooting if they play games; also, begs the question as to what qualifies as *violent*).

3. False dilemma/poisoning the well/slippery slope (more than one choice possible; also, makes Republicans look bad; implies that just voting for a Republican will cause taxes for military spending).

4. Begging the question (question is, is there a "best" baby?). It is also false analogy (can one compare an object like a car to a baby)?

5. False analogy/slippery slope (baby's being compared again; also there is definitely nothing that will *prevent* us from ever "repeating" some mistake).

6. Begging the question/post hoc (implies that there is something he doesn't want her to hear and suggests he hung up because she came in, so this is post hoc).

7. Begging the question (do we "all know that?"). This assumes a fact not in evidence.

8. Ad hominem/begging the question/epithet (character attack and labeling him a coward).

9. Slippery slope/poisoning the well/ad hominem. (The chief can't be certain the community will cry out; he's also publicly assassinating the character of the accused, so it is both ad hominem and poisoning the well, since it's before an audience.)

10. Begging the question/equivocating. (Were *handguns* in schools during the Columbine attacks or other shootings? No. The word "guns" is being used ambiguously, so we have equivocation.)

11. Poisoning the well/ad hominem/slippery slope/begging the question/epithet (making the teacher look bad in front of an audience while attacking him personally; also claiming that something is going to occur that probably is not, just as a result of this case). Begs the question, "Is science godless?" If you read the play or watch the film *Inherit the Wind*, you will see this claim about scientists made, i.e., that they don't believe in God and are all atheists.

CHAPTER SEVEN

Readings for Critical Analysis

Author's note: Below is an article I published in a Hayward, California paper (*The Daily Review*) after the 1992 Rodney King riots. I have changed it significantly for the purposes of this book! Refer to the author as me, Debra Stevens. I was very pleased, by the way, that they put this editorial right next to Mike Royko's. However, I didn't like the cartoon graphic they included of a child staring up-close at a television set. Kind of misdirected my readers. Oh well. You decide what my question at issue here is.

TV and Movies Distort Reality

The television and movie media are spinning out of control. Hiding behind the First Amendment to the U.S. Constitution, the media have been presenting material for us to consume, or perhaps choke on.

For the past twenty years that I can recall, Americans have been subjected to a worsening diet of television and movie violence. No amount of violence has been too much to expect us to consume, no kind of violence was considered too raw to offer up.

Media handling of the news is often overdone, terrifying at times, and is often also a matter of speculation: They select, slant, and omit certain events, discuss simplistic possibilities as facts, come up with half-baked cause-effect relationships, and we swallow it down, or in some cases even cough it back up to our colleagues at work, suggesting that what was really just speculation is in fact a fact. The media allows politicians and concerned social scientists to voice opinions that sound factual, and the public is led to believe fiction is truth, or that the media does indeed have the full story, when indeed they do not.

This combination of a diet of violence and ignorance causes us to react, judge, and fear, not think independently and respond wisely.

Take for instance the Rodney King case. What was the television media's role in that? If the media wanted to aggrandize itself and focus attention on itself so as to get lots and lots of advertising revenue, what would it do?

First, we have to backtrack and realize that the television programmers are playing to the same crowd that has been conditioned by the movie media. That's the media that has traditionally shown class against class, race against race, simple bad guys fighting other simple bad guys. The filmmakers have usually thrown into the mix a couple of positive stories showing racial harmony, some good guys, a black and a white cop working together or something simple like that. To fend off critics and parents, the movie media has interspersed a few stories like *White Men Can't Jump, Dangerous Minds,* and *American History X,* but no serious discourse on racial differences has ever been put forward by the large movie studios. *American History X* comes close, but many people find it too vulgar, too harsh. As a matter of fact, some other people would find pseudo-harmonizing irritating and vulgar, or even idiotic.

As for violence, they would be free to show anything and everything in close-up detail. Murders, rapes, tortures, you name it. They would present violent stories in as simplistic a fashion as possible. Killers with no remorse would be glorified on the big screen. I hardly need to give any illustrations of such movies, but just in case you can't think of any, how about *The Godfather?* People loved that movie and idolized the hero, who was, after all, a murderer.

The television media could thus defend criticism of its close-up coverage of tragedies, its barrage of stories about shootings and crimes. It would defend its coverage of sensational stories like its Sunday morning coverage of a pregnant woman jumping out of a ten-story window. The television media would defend this by one simple idea: "They love it. The audience wants it. *They* tune in. We just produce it. They consume it. They ask for it."

The outcome? For the media, lots and lots of sales. For the public? A feeling that the world is an awful and dangerous place. Also, since most of the crimes in the news involve people other than white people, a connection is made. The stage is set for a social explosion of bad reasoning and finger-pointing, and some indifference to violence. False beliefs and gullibility abound.

With all of this in the background, in the minds of the watchers, what happens after the TV media repeatedly shows the Rodney King beating?

The media shows it more times than they showed the Challenger going down, so the black community is repeatedly targeted, invigorated, and incensed.

Next step: Show people talking on talk shows, lots of white people, actually, discussing black people's discontent and the reasons for this. Have other videos of other cases where police violence and unreasonable use of force is evident. Don't stress differences in circumstances. Don't discuss the particulars of the Rodney King case. Pick up footage that is sensational and inflammatory.

What would be the outcome? For the media, you guessed it, more people tuning in—and more money. For us? Those predisposed to negative racial views would be primed and infuriated. Hatred toward cops would be exposed and nurtured. Some people would find more reason to fear cops. (Later on, ironically, there would be more cop shows.)

What would the media do next? It would lay down the fuse and hand us the match, release the jury verdict and show it repeatedly. They would give no background for this besides clips of outraged black people and inarticulate white people on the street. People interviewed would be (guess what?) predicting a riot. Hey, the fuse is lit!

The first major explosion that night booms out of L.A., and the fire spreads across the United States. What now? It seems like things are going pretty well. What else can the media possibly do? Show the riot footage again and again. Don't show any Asian or white people looting, just blacks. Top it off with psychologists speculating, police personnel trying to explain away the whole thing, feebly, of course. Broadcast how the mayor dropped the ball. Show the people in the streets running out of convenience stores with six-packs. Yeah, get a shot of that guy running in the street with the television! (Were there any black people during this riot not participating, condemning this aspect of the riot? Who knew? Not the American public.)

Does the media control us, or do we control it? How many times will it take before we turn the damn thing off? Car commercials, two every eight minutes, simple stories of unfunny white people and bad news are everywhere. What is the damn thing good for? Throw it out and retrieve your dignity. If you want some news, pick up a newspaper. We want responsible journalism, right? We don't need sensationalism in our news to brighten up our dreary lives. We don't need our kids watching violence on "the news." We need to protect our children of every race. We have the right to be treated like intelligent human beings, but not until we take back those rights from the false educators called the television media.

Tommy's Story by D. Stevens

The woman in this story is I, about fifteen years ago. You'll see me, sitting and staring at a soiled dining room tablecloth, ignoring my child, diligently studying, bent over doing research on fallacious reasoning for a thesis I was constructing for the English department at UC Berkeley. Like I said, you'll see me ignoring this child, this baby of three with his angel baby blond hair and round greenish eyes until I can't see straight anymore. Try not to judge me too harshly. I'm like most of us, easily distracted. So, I interrupted my studies, my research into *logos*, because little, 34" Tommy said . . .

"I'm not sleepy. I'm not tired, Mommy. I can watch TV now. I can sit here and . . ." Tommy was out of the bedroom again, pulling my shirt and pointing at the television set, which was off, and looking up wide-eyed, right into my face, staring straight into my eyes, and I swear at that time I realized I could hardly see him even though he was only less than a foot from me. When I realized I was unable to focus on him, I concentrated on his voice, the feeling of it. He pulled me back to the present. He was pleading with me just to turn on the television. I felt his loneliness. That feeling inserted itself and made guilt well up. (Was this *guilt appeal*? I wondered.) This in turn caused me to consider turning on the television for my three-year-old, which in turn caused more guilt, which caused me to stop and look at the whole scene, take my head out of my books and focus on him, the little . . . (This was not the first time he would do this to me. Oh no, this is still going on. He pulls me away from where I'm headed and makes me see just him and what he needs. Yes, I know this is *begging the question.* It was all up to me. I made my own choices.) But anyway, back to Tommy . . .

"I don't want you to watch too much television. It's bad for you. Still, I have to work now." He didn't budge. He just slobbered on his thumb. There was no reasoning with this kid!

"Read me a story. Read me, read me . . . REEEEAD MEEE . . ." "I can't right now."

I heard myself say this and considered briefly just how much time I had already spent just discussing the possibility of his doing something and how much thought I had put into this problem and knew that this was going to turn into one of those protracted discussions where I would eventually put down what I wanted to do and do what he wanted me to do. (Like I said, this still goes on.) I was worried and thought, "I will never get this work done if I don't do it now." Then I realized that was *slippery slope*!

I looked long and hard at the top of his fine, curly head as he held my leg. I considered what I could do as a sort of a compromise, meaning what I could sort of half do with him and half do for me so I could continue to work. Now *that*, I knew, was *begging the question*, but I tried it anyway. Like I said, I was still studying logic.

"I have an idea. You tell me a story." ("There," I thought. "That will occupy him!") I walked over and turned up the heater. It was freezing all of a sudden. Then I put a beanbag chair down next to my chair, got him a blanket, and told him to sit there and think of a story. "Okay," I said to myself, sitting back at the table, staring at the piles of books, "that should do it!"

It didn't. He wanted me. He wanted *me*. Thus he decided to pull out the big guns. After sitting and frowning at his feet for a while, he countered, "You tell me a story. Make it up. Make up a story and you tell *me* a story. You tell *good* stories. Tell me a *new* story. Please!"

This three-year-old, I swear, knew how to appeal to my ego. I've already told you that I was studying for a graduate degree in English. That's because I wanted to teach eventually. Why? I had once wanted to write. All of you ex-English majors know what I'm talking about. Writing, I felt, was too lofty and remote a possibility for lowly old me. So I of course sought out and won a teaching position. I never published a thing. Well, I did eventually get that thesis published. But anyway . . .

This was tough thinking. I could feel myself aging. Gray hairs, I knew, were beginning to form. This must stop, but what to do? This little tyrant, with his curly hair and angelic face, knew my psyche and knew I loved to create and to write and would instantly stop what I was doing and right there compose a story with him, probably with him in my lap, where my books should have been. He knew it, and he was right, and soon he was very secure there in my lap, with that smile and those big green or blue, whatever, eyes. He had me by the intellect . . . and I was pleased. I was calm. What was wrong with me? Where were my loyalties?

Thus it came to be that, together, in my bedroom, under the covers, in a makeshift cave, the story of the frogs unfolded. I asked him questions, he answered. Then he asked me questions. I answered. We made the story of the frogs that hopped out of our minds and into a cave looking for shelter from the impending ice age. To keep from becoming frogsicles, the frogs had packed all of their family pictures and brought their rocks and sticks and everything into the cave, but they were in the dark so they had to figure out how to get light in the cave and they reasoned that they couldn't use fire because it would cause a lot of smoke, so they had to think of some other source of light. They thought about kicking holes in the ceiling of the cave, but then ice would fall through. So they thought and thought (meaning Tommy thought and thought) and eventually came up with the idea of capturing fireflies on the tips of their tongues and using these as lights, which meant that they had to live, in the night time, with their tongues hanging out all the time, which made it hard to croak and eat, but at least they could see. And then there was the added bonus of being able to eat your little illuminating insect when you wanted to close your eyes and just go to sleep in your cave with your family. Some of the fireflies were not eaten but kept in a little rock-enclosed space like a fort. They were spares. Some of the frogs hung their family pictures on the cave walls and stuck fireflies all around the frames, so there was always some light and so the frogs could put their tongues back in their mouths. In the evenings there were always smiling, happy, frog family faces glowing down at them. And so they slept in their cave during the ice age, and Tommy took his nap, with his mom's arms around him, because she had no willpower and still doesn't really have much where he is concerned because she probably loves him more than, well, most other things. I know. It doesn't make any sense, but I think if you really think about it, most things that really matter to us don't. I wonder why that is?

The end

Massaab by Basudha Sengupta (short story)

Along with an insipid taste in my mouth, as I was looking through my window, I suddenly felt a sharp twitch in my left ear. My left hand automatically reached the ear and caressed it smoothly. This twitch took me back to my childhood days, to the age of nine when I was determined to avenge myself on my private tutor, Massaab, who without any qualms punished us severely.

My elder sister, Didi, and I sat with Massaab daily for two hours at the grand oak oval table doing our homework under his strict supervision, which was intermittently interrupted by unwarranted showers of sudden smacks leaving imprints of his fingers right on our tender cheeks, or rampant pulling of our ears over our slightest sloppy errors. He clenched his fists and beat them against our backs or even heads without any remorse.

I was an average child with simple pranks and innocent tricks up my sleeves at times to tease my teachers or irritate my elders whenever I got bored or whenever I wanted some attention.

I was somewhat of a *phankibaj*, slyly neglectful girl. I often finished my work with minimum effort. I had no grand goals ahead of me, nor was I very studious. Playful and adventurous, I was a proud girl with some vague convictions of my own and a common sense of self-esteem and dignity. However, Ma was never satisfied with my schoolwork. She wanted me to do far better. "Study hard. Good results are your only hope." With these mantras, Ma tried to instruct us; however, she was always entangled with her unending, tedious household chores. I often took advantage of her tight schedule. Sneaking out and playing with neighborhood kids were my most prized achievements.

Ours was an extended family. My sister, Didi, and I lived with Dadu, our grandfather, Thakuma, our grandmother, Baba, our father, Shankar, our youngest brother, and those innumerable guests who kept us busy with their unannounced frequent visits and their weeklong stays. Pishi, our father's youngest sister, came with her two children whenever she got bored in her house. Our two bachelor uncles often dropped in addressing my mother: "Bowdie! Here is your favorite fish." Along with fresh produce, goat meat and other cooking ingredients, they frolicked into our home whenever they felt like it. Though we all ate and enjoyed our mother's cooking, no one ever thought how extra hard Mother had to work.

These guests were a great relief to Didi and me. They gave us excuses for not doing our homework or studies. Our guests aggravated Ma's silent displeasure. We had to be polite, talk to them, and share our company. If we failed to do so, we were disrespectful, selfish, callous, or impolite. How could we concede to such titles?

Didi and I always greeted their arrivals, but we were fearful of their departure. As soon as they left, Ma would burst with anger and ask us to show our homework, often incomplete or filled with errors. She would retaliate and with her stern voice say, "Just like others. When will you both be responsible and do your tasks? The doors of this house will ever remain open for the guests whether I like it or not. Who cares for my opinion? Now, like them, you too have started ignoring my wishes. I expect at least my daughters will be wise enough to do their studies. Forget about helping me with my household work." We took her speech, her litany, as a harangue.

Our guests and their disrespect for any schedule made Ma very unhappy. But, like all mothers, she always had solutions to all kinds of problems, no matter how trivial or serious they were.

One day Ma got a private tutor for us whom we called with utmost respect Massaab. Our parents and grandparents also called him Massaab. To both of us he was an old man with a rickety frame, always in his white spotless *dhoti* and *kurta*, a typical Indian male outfit.

Except Sundays, Massaab came to our house every day as sure as death. At the stroke of six, he was ever present at the door. Often we had seen Ma setting the kitchen wall clock with his arrival. Thus he maintained his punctuality to impose his blind adherence to strict discipline. He rode his bike (that too was rickety like his frail yet erect body), riding approximately four or five miles one way to our house.

Massaab resembled a dried-up stick, lifeless and hard with no room for any compassion or remorse; rather, he was robotic to the nth degree. Each day he came, checked our work, and prepared us for our next day's school assignment or any upcoming test. Every day he dictated fifty words for spelling. One error and a smack on my cheek was his way to reinforce correct spelling. I wanted to write stories out of my vocabulary list, but such freedom to him was promoting promiscuous imagination, not healthy for a growing child. Holding our reader nearly ten to twelve inches away from my eyes and standing straight on both legs and reading the story aloud was a regimented routine that I detested. There was no variety, no fun in his teaching. His patent and monotonous assignments were one page of Hindi and one page of English handwriting, writing the tables from two to twenty, and writing down the numbers from one to one hundred every day. For English handwriting practice we had to write this sentence: "God is good." I never knew, while Massaab was with us, how God could be good because Massaab's presence was a dreadful, two-hour torturous feat. For Hindi we had to write in Devnagri script "Ram is a good boy" (Ram, the hero of our sacred epic *The Ramayana*). For some strange reason, we were never given the option to write "Sita [Ram's consort] is a good girl."

Day in and day out, we had to do the same task. We snickered behind him and called him and his assignments "dried sticks." Massaab would diligently check our homework, ask questions, help us memorize poems, and prepare us for our school. Didi and I had no problem in doing our schoolwork, but Massaab's assignments were tedious and uninspiring. Unlike other friends, Didi and I were overburdened with a double load of homework. It seemed Ma and Massaab had conspired together against us. We were the innocent little lambs now left with no more excuses or choice, but left to our fate to withstand the upcoming onslaughts.

Massaab seemed invincible. He never fell sick. He was never absent, for no misfortune would interrupt his routine schedule at our house. Maybe he was powerless to resist the magnetic force that pulled him toward our house every day around six in the evening, as if the magnetic current automatically got activated by some mysterious agent.

The first two years were uneventful, writing those murderous, meaningless sentences. After school, every day I played with my neighborhood friends in our front yard, where Dadu sat with watchful eyes on our activities. When Ma from the kitchen called, "Chatu, stop your games and come in right away. Massaab will be in any minute," my heart pounded because I hadn't done my two pages of handwriting nor written the multiplication tables. I fruitlessly prayed the clock to stop, but as ruthless and heartless as time is, it never showed any mercy or consideration. Time steadily continued to tick and moved forward. God only knew what time had up its sleeves. My last resort was a painful plea. "Ma, my tummy hurts. Oh! I can't sit."

Very patiently Ma would reply, "Well, just put your homework on the table for Massaab to check. I'll ask him to excuse you for tonight. You can go to bed."

Massaab believed in corporal punishment to keep his students in line. As we grew older, and the third year rolled on, Massaab became very tough. At the sight of a slight error, with unexpected suddenness he would pull my ears or squeeze my earlobe between his thumb and index finger, or smack my face faster than lightning, often bringing uncontrollable tears rolling down my cheeks. This was his way of setting things straight, and probably some kind of a strange stimulation he got out of his beatings. Didi was treated in the same manner; however, Didi was made of different elements than I. She had a different attitude altogether about Massaab's abuse. She was not openly defiant or defensive about this situation. Rather she remained callous, stubborn, and absolutely cold. Later, as his spanking and smacking continued, I, too, became numb to what he did. My silence was an affront to his authority and it provoked him to use more force. The more he twisted my cheeks or ears, the harder I tried to control my muscles. After a while my muscles got accustomed to these hard blows and twists, and I literally didn't feel any pain. I never cried again nor did tears ever roll down my cheeks.

"Ma, Massaab hits us. You must tell him not to smack us" failed to convince her. "Concentrate on your work and try not to make any mistakes. You're punished for your carelessness," the usual response came from her. Perhaps Ma felt that her incorrigible daughters were being justly disciplined by Massaab.

Since there were no encouraging responses from Ma, and Massaab's tortures increased heavily, I decided to avenge myself on Massaab. Whenever he hit me, I felt humiliated; my dignity was stolen; my identity was violated.

I declared a silent war. I accepted his challenge. I did my homework that I had to do. I prepared my lessons with minor errors here and there that could have been rectified. The slightest mistakes or error became a strategic target for him to use his force ruthlessly.

Around seven we used to have a short stretch break for ten or fifteen minutes. We'd go to the bathroom, or drink water, or just roam around the house stretching while Massaab savored the snack that Ma had sent in for him. It was a ritual for Ma. "Chatu, come. The tea is ready." The tea was always served with a plate filled with snacks like flat biscuits or spicy fresh fried pakoras.

While I went into the kitchen to fetch the goodies, I surreptitiously licked those biscuits or sipped the hot Darjeeling tea with its perfect blend of sugar and cream. While I sipped or licked, a sacrilegious act, a wild sensation flowed through my body. I performed this sneaky trick a few more times.

However, it wouldn't retain its charm. I lost interest in this device. My heart wasn't contented with such a mild form of revenge. I promised myself, "No more licking, no more sipping." Revenge has to be formidable, whereas mine was heading toward a gentle absurdity. My revenge had to match Massaab's intensity, or his callous ruthlessness toward my feelings. We had to be equal rivals. I became adamant. A little imp was about to be released from a sorcerer's bottle.

Now, my childlike revenge was heading toward strategic offensive tactics. I had to do something that would hurt Massaab physically. However, I was glad, later, to find out that his hurt extended to monetary hassle as well. That was not included in my plan, but I was proud to be discreet and innovative in my adroit maneuver.

That rickety bike became my prime target. Yes, that was the real mechanism that transported Massaab daily to our house. That bike should be destroyed. I became the solitary soldier in charge of the plot and its execution. In war you can't even trust your own blood. I didn't say a word to Didi. Didi's non-aggressiveness was disturbing for me. It meant I must venture alone with my secret plan.

It was a cold December night. Ma and Baba had gone to the community club for their regular Saturday meeting. Thakuma and Dadu had gone to visit their youngest son who had bought a new house in the city.

Our house was one of the military single barracks constructed during World War II, nearly twenty miles away from the conveniences of city life with no public transportation and with very limited facilities. Apart from the main streets connecting different barracks, the roads were neither paved nor lit. Consequently, those unpaved dirt roads that wandered and crisscrossed through the corn or rice fields or barren lands, leading toward the outskirts of the village where Massaab came from were shrouded with the darkness on that cold December night.

Usually winter nights were deserted. After the sunset, no one would be about, save someone like Massaab. Only a sudden squall of wind would disturb the silence of the languid night, accompanied perhaps by the hooting of an owl or the thrashing of a wayward animal trying to hide in the bushes after being attacked. As usual, Massaab came at six. He parked his bike under the verandah roof.

Once he was inside our study room, the door behind him was closed so that the cold wind could not cross the room. The tiny forty-watt bulb was trying to drive off the encroaching darkness. That night, to facilitate my movements, I sneaked out and turned off the light. It was pitch dark. Just a faint streak of light from the room had unintentionally pierced through the window crack. That minute streak was more than sufficient for my job.

It was a perfect night that urged me to muster up my courage. Today, I had to prepare the tea for Massaab as Ma was not home. Today's break was obviously going to be a long one for me. After giving him his tea, I asked Massaab to let me go to the toilet to do my urgent big job. As usual, he sipped his tea and enjoyed his snacks.

I went to the backyard and gathered my weapons. They were nearly four inches long, pointed heavy-duty nails, not rusty, but clean and new. I had taken them from Dadu's toolbox. After his retirement, Dadu had become the family handyman; he had a toolbox, filled with different shapes and sizes of nails and other handy gadgets. It was a treasure box for me. I quietly sneaked to the front door where the bike was stationed.

Three nails secured and stored in my skirt pocket, I held one nail in my hand like a dagger. With a vicious smile on my face, pursing my lips, I snarled my contempt by jabbing furiously the front tire with the nail. Then I repeated the same steps with the other tire; I was jabbing over and over again until the air was gone. Momentarily, I felt dizzy. I kept on jabbing. Although it was cold, my palms and forehead felt sweaty. The savage attack must have lasted four to five minutes. I soon hurled those nails at the dark night, scattering them into the open fields, never to be found again.

At this point, I couldn't afford to lose my calm. Straight away I headed toward the toilet, stayed there for a few minutes, flushed the toilet for authenticity. I cleansed my hands in the nearby washbasin. Lifting the hem of my skirt, as I was wiping my hands, I entered the room with a sense of power and victory.

Seeing me lifting my skirt up, Massaab yelled, "Put down your skirt," and with a jolt pulled my right ear.

"Never lift your skirt in front of others, you indecent fool."

Today I was oblivious of his instructions. I was waiting for Massaab to go home. Finally, he left the chair. I jumped out of my chair because suddenly every moment fell heavy on my heart. I folded my palms together and lifted them up to my chin level as though before the Lord to say my prayers, to say goodbye. Didi opened the door for him and Massaab walked toward his parked bike.

Since I had turned off the light, I went to the switch and turned on the light so that he could see his bike. The forty-watt bulb, as our night guard, wasn't bright enough to let us see things clearly. Massaab pulled his bike forward, but the bike felt heavy to him. He bent forward to feel the tire by giving it a sturdy squeeze at which he was quite proficient. The tire felt flat; the same with the rear tire. He nodded his head and irritably said, "Hey Ram. Tires are flat." Happily, we didn't have any spare bike or air pump for his immediate rescue; moreover, Ma and Baba were not home.

With a pitiless glitter in my eyes, I saw Massaab dragging his bike, disappearing into the misty winter fog, and my heart ached with a vicious joy.

Communication: Its Blocking and Its Facilitation by Carl Rogers

The whole task of psychotherapy is the task of dealing with a failure in communication. The emotionally maladjusted person, the "neurotic," is in difficulty first because communication within himself has broken down, and second because as a result of this, his communication with others has been damaged. As long as this is true, there are distortions in the way he communicates himself to others, and so he suffers both within himself, and in his interpersonal relations. The task of psychotherapy is to help the person achieve, through a special relationship with a therapist, good communication within himself. Once this is achieved he can communicate more freely and more effectively with others. We may say then that psychotherapy is good communication, within and between men. We may also turn that statement around and it will still be true. Good communication, free communication, within or between men, is always therapeutic.

It is, then, from a background of experience with communication in counseling and psychotherapy that I want to present here two ideas. I wish to state what I believe is one of the major factors in or impeding communication, and then I wish to present what in our experience has proven to be a very important way of improving or facilitating communication.

I would like to propose, as a hypothesis for consideration, that the major barrier to mutual interpersonal communication is our very natural tendency to judge, to evaluate, to approve or disapprove, the statement of the other person, or the other group. Let me illustrate my meaning with some very simple examples. As you leave a lecture meeting, one of the statements you are likely to hear is, "1 didn't like that man's talk." Now what do you respond? Almost invariably your reply will be either approval or disapproval of the attitude expressed. Either you respond, "I didn't either. I thought it was terrible," or else you tend to reply, "Oh, I thought it was really good." In other words, your primary reaction is to evaluate what has just been said to you, to evaluate it from your point of view, your own frame of reference.

This brings in another element connected with my hypothesis. Although the tendency to make evaluations is common in almost all interchange of language, it is very much heightened in those situations where feelings and emotions are deeply involved. So the stronger our feelings, the more likely it is that there will be no mutual element in the communication. I'm sure you recognize this from your own experience. When you have not been emotionally involved yourself, and have listened to a heated discussion, you often go away thinking, "Well, they actually weren't talking about the same thing." And they were not. Each was making a judgment, an evaluation, from his own frame of reference. There was really nothing which could be called communication in any genuine sense. This tendency to react to any emotionally meaningful statement by forming an evaluation of it from our own point of view is, I repeat, the major barrier to interpersonal communication.

But is there any way of solving this problem, of avoiding this barrier? Real communication occurs, and this evaluative tendency is avoided, when we listen with understanding. What does this mean? It means to *see the expressed idea and attitude from the other person's point of view,* to *sense how it feels* to him, to *achieve* his *frame of reference in regard* to *the thing* he is *talking about.*

Stated so briefly, this may sound absurdly simple, but it is not. It is an approach which we have found extremely potent in the field of psychotherapy. It is the most effective agent we know for altering the basic personality structure of an individual and improving his relationships and his communications with others. If I can listen to what he can tell me, if I can understand how it seems to him, if I can see its personal meaning for him, if I can sense the emotional flavor which it has for him, then I will be releasing potent forces of change in him. We know from our research that such empathic understanding *with* a person, not *about* him is such an effective approach that it can bring about major changes in personality.

Some of you may be feeling that you listen well to people, and that you have never seen such results. The chances are very great indeed that your listening has not been of the type I have described. Fortunately, I can suggest a little laboratory experiment which you can try to test the quality of your understanding. The next time you get into an argument with your wife, or your friend, or with a small group of friends, just stop the discussion a moment and for an experiment, institute this test. Each person can speak up for himself only when he has first restated the ideas and feelings of the previous speaker accurately, and to that speaker's satisfaction. You see what this would mean. It would simply mean that before presenting your own point of view, it would be necessary for you to really achieve the other speaker's frame of reference to understand his thoughts and feelings so well that you could summarize them for him. Sounds simple, doesn't it? But if you try it you will discover it is one of the most difficult things you have ever tried to do. However, once you have been able to see the other's point of view, your own comments will have to be drastically revised. You will also find the emotion going out of the discussion, the differences being reduced, and those differences which remain being of a rational and understandable sort.

If, then, this way of approach is an effective avenue to good communication and good relationships, why is it not more widely tried and used? I will try to list the difficulties which keep it from being utilized.

In the first place it takes courage, a quality which is not too widespread. I am indebted to Dr. S. I. Hayakawa, the semanticist, for pointing out that to carry on psychotherapy in this fashion is to take a very real risk, and that courage is required. If you really understand another person in this way, if you are willing to enter his private world and see the way life appears to him without any attempt to make evaluative judgments, you run the risk of being changed yourself. You might see it his way, you might find yourself influenced in your attitudes or your personality. This risk of being changed is one of the most frightening prospects most of us can face.

But there is a second obstacle. It is just when emotions are strongest that it is most difficult to achieve the frame of reference of the other person or group. Yet it is the time the attitude is most needed, if communication is to be established. We have not found this to be an insuperable obstacle in our experience in psychotherapy. A third party, who is able to lay aside his own feelings and evaluations, can assist greatly by listening with understanding to each person or group and clarifying the views and attitudes each holds. We have found this very effective in small groups in which contradictory or antagonistic attitudes exist. When the parties to a dispute realize that they are being understood, that someone sees how the situation seems to them, the statements grow less exaggerated and less defensive, and it is no longer necessary to maintain the attitude, "I am 100 percent right and you are 100 percent wrong." The influence of such an understanding catalyst in the group permits the members to come closer and closer to the objective truth involved in the relationship. In this way mutual communication is established and some type of agreement becomes much more possible.

In closing, I would like to summarize this small-scale solution to the problem of barriers in communication, and to point out certain of its characteristics.

I have said that our research and experience to date would make it appear that breakdowns in communication, and the evaluative tendency which is the major barrier to communication, can be avoided. The solution is provided by creating a situation in which each of the different parties comes to understand the other from the *other's* point of view. This has been achieved, in practice, even when feelings run high, by the influence of a person who is willing to understand each point of view empathically, and who thus acts as a catalyst to precipitate further understanding.

This procedure has important characteristics. It can be initiated by one party, without waiting for the other to be ready. It can even be initiated by a neutral person, providing he can gain a minimum of cooperation from one of the parties.

This procedure can deal with the insincerities, the defensive exaggerations, the lies, the "false fronts" which characterize almost every failure in communication. These defensive distortions drop away with astonishing speed as people find that the only intent is to understand, not judge.

This approach leads steadily and rapidly toward the discovery of the truth, toward a realistic appraisal of the objective barriers to communication. The dropping of some defensiveness by one party leads to further dropping of defensiveness by the other party, and truth is thus approached.

This procedure gradually achieves mutual communication. Mutual communication tends to be pointed toward solving a problem rather than toward attacking a person or group. It leads to a situation in which I see how the problem appears to you, as well as to me, and you see how it appears to me, as well as to you. Thus accurately and realistically defined, the problem is almost certain to yield to intelligent attack, or if it is in part insoluble, it will be comfortably accepted as such.

Allegory of the Cave

The Allegory of the Cave is part of Book VII of Plato's Republic, *reproduced in its entirety below. In it, Socrates elucidates some ideas we have been considering ever since reading Chapter One of Making Sense, ideas concerning observing objectively, seeing only what is there and questioning what is not there. We learned that as new critical thinkers, we are becoming more and more aware of habits that are barriers to objective reasoning, critical thinking, barriers that Carl Rogers spoke of in his article about communication.*

An allegory is an anecdote that relies on symbols and imagery to make an abstract concept concrete. Each of the elements of the allegorical scene represents something. The cave, sun, cave dwellers and their poor vision, shadows and more should be considered as symbols and discussed as to their most reasonable interpretation. Readers can draw reasonable inferences, based on their critical analysis, as to Socrates' overall meaning, what he hopes Glaucon will learn from the example. At the end of the allegory, Socrates tries to help his young student, Glaucon, apply the lesson to the political situation in Athens and to see a distinction between philosophers and politicians; as in so many other dialogues concerning what is "good" or beneficial for people living together in communities, Socrates sees good individuals seeking truth and understanding are hard to find, but they are the only ones we should want leading us. The question arises, of course, just how will those whom are not yet enlightened recognize the truth spoken by such individuals? Is there a situation in our own time to which we could reasonably apply this lesson?

[**Socrates**] And now, I said, let me show in a figure how far our nature is enlightened or unenlightened:

—Behold! human beings living in a underground cave, which has a mouth open towards the light and reaching all along the cave; here they have been from their childhood, and have their legs and necks chained so that they cannot move, and can only see before them, being prevented by the chains from turning round their heads. Above and behind them a fire is blazing at a distance, and between the fire and the prisoners there is a raised way; and you will see, if you look, a low wall built along the way, like the screen which marionette players have in front of them, over which they show the puppets.

[Glaucon] I see.

[Socrates] And do you see, I said, men passing along the wall carrying all sorts of vessels, and statues and figures of animals made of wood and stone and various materials, which appear over the wall? Some of them are talking, others silent.

[Glaucon] You have shown me a strange image, and they are strange prisoners.

[Socrates] Like ourselves, I replied; and they see only their own shadows, or the shadows of one another, which the fire throws on the opposite wall of the cave?

[Glaucon] True, he said; how could they see anything but the shadows if they were never allowed to move their heads?

[Socrates] And of the objects which are being carried in like manner they would only see the shadows?

[Glaucon] Yes, he said.

[Socrates] And if they were able to converse with one another, would they not suppose that they were naming what was actually before them?

[Glaucon] Very true.

[Socrates] And suppose further that the prison had an echo which came from the other side, would they not be sure to fancy when one of the passers-by spoke that the voice which they heard came from the passing shadow?

[Glaucon] No question, he replied.

[Socrates] To them, I said, the truth would be literally nothing but the shadows of the images.

[Glaucon] That is certain.

[Socrates] And now look again, and see what will naturally follow if the prisoners are released and disabused of their error. At first, when any of them is liberated and compelled suddenly to stand up and turn his neck round and walk and look towards the light, he will suffer sharp pains; the glare will distress him, and he will be unable to see the realities of which in his former state he had seen the shadows; and then conceive some one saying to him, that what he saw before was an illusion, but that now, when he is approaching nearer to being and his eye is turned towards more real existence, he has a clearer vision, what will be his reply? And you may further imagine that his instructor is pointing to the objects as they pass and requiring him to name them, will he not be perplexed? Will he not fancy that the shadows which he formerly saw are truer than the objects which are now shown to him?

[**Glaucon**] Far truer.

[**Socrates**] And if he is compelled to look straight at the light, will he not have a pain in his eyes which will make him turn away to take and take in the objects of vision which he can see, and which he will conceive to be in reality clearer than the things which are now being shown to him?

[**Glaucon**] True, he now.

[**Socrates**] And suppose once more, that he is reluctantly dragged up a steep and rugged ascent, and held fast until he's forced into the presence of the sun himself, is he not likely to be pained and irritated? When he approaches the light his eyes will be dazzled, and he will not be able to see anything at all of what are now called realities.

[**Glaucon**] Not all in a moment, he said.

[**Socrates**] He will be required to grow accustomed to the sight of the upper world. And first he will see the shadows best, next the reflections of men and other objects in the water, and then the objects themselves; then he will gaze upon the light of the moon and the stars and the spangled heaven; and he will see the sky and the stars by night better than the sun or the light of the sun by day?

[**Glaucon**] Certainly.

[**Socrates**] Last of he will be able to see the sun, and not mere reflections of him in the water, but he will see him in his own proper place, and not in another; and he will contemplate him as he is.

[**Glaucon**] Certainly.

[**Socrates**] He will then proceed to argue that this is he who gives the season and the years, and is the guardian of all that is in the visible world, and in a certain way the cause of all things which he and his fellows have been accustomed to behold?

[**Glaucon**] Clearly, he said, he would first see the sun and then reason about him.

[**Socrates**] And when he remembered his old habitation, and the wisdom of the cave and his fellow-prisoners, do you not suppose that he would felicitate himself on the change, and pity them?

[**Glaucon**] Certainly, he would.

[**Socrates**] And if they were in the habit of conferring honors among themselves on those who were quickest to observe the passing shadows and to remark which of them went before, and which followed after, and which were together; and who were therefore best able to draw conclusions as to the future, do you think that he would care for such honors and glories, or envy the possessors of them? Would he not say with Homer.

Better to be the poor servant of a poor master,

and to endure anything, rather than think as they do and live after their manner?

[**Glaucon**] Yes, he said, I think that he would rather suffer anything than entertain these false notions and live in this miserable manner.

[**Socrates**] Imagine once more, I said, such an one coming suddenly out of the sun to be replaced in his old situation; would he not be certain to have his eyes full of darkness?

[**Glaucon**] To be sure, he said.

[**Socrates**] And if there were a contest, and he had to compete in measuring the shadows with the prisoners who had never moved out of the cave, while his sight was still weak, and before his eyes had become steady (and the time which would be needed to acquire this new habit of sight might be very considerable) would he not be ridiculous? Men would say of him that up he went and down he came without his eyes; and that it was better not even to think of ascending; and if any one tried to loose another and lead him up to the light, let them only catch the offender, and they would put him to death.

[**Glaucon**] No question, he said.

[**Socrates**] This entire allegory, I said, you may now append, dear Glaucon, to the previous argument; the prison-house is the world of sight, the light of the fire is the sun, and you will not misapprehend me if you interpret the journey upwards to be the ascent of the soul into the intellectual world according to my poor belief, which, at your desire, I have expressed whether rightly or wrongly God knows. But, whether true or false, my opinion is that in the world of knowledge the idea of good appears last of all, and is seen only with an effort; and, when seen, is also inferred to be the universal author of all things beautiful and right, parent of light and of the lord of light in this visible world, and the immediate source of reason and truth in the intellectual; and that this is the power upon which he who would act rationally, either in public or private life must have his eye fixed.

[**Glaucon**] I agree, he said, as far as I am able to understand you.

[**Socrates**] Moreover, I said, you must not wonder that those who attain to this beatific vision are unwilling to descend to human affairs; for their souls are ever hastening into the upper world where they desire to dwell; which desire of theirs is very natural, if our allegory may be trusted.

[**Glaucon**] Yes, very natural.

[**Socrates**] And is there anything surprising in one who passes from divine contemplations to the evil state of man, misbehaving himself in a ridiculous manner; if, while his eyes are blinking and before he has become accustomed to the surrounding darkness, he is compelled to fight in courts of law, or in other places, about the images or the shadows of images of justice, and is endeavoring to meet the conceptions of those who have never yet seen absolute justice?

[**Glaucon**] Anything but surprising, he replied.

[**Socrates**] Any one who has common sense will remember that the bewilderments of the eyes are of two kinds, and arise from two causes, either from coming out of the light or from going into the light, which is true of the mind's eye, quite as much as of the bodily eye; and he who remembers this when he sees any one whose vision is perplexed and weak, will not be too ready to laugh; he will first ask whether that soul of man has come out of the brighter light, and is unable to see because unaccustomed to the dark, or having turned from darkness to the day is dazzled by excess of light. And he will count the one happy in his condition and state of being, and he will pity the other; or, if he have a mind to laugh at the soul which comes from below into the light, there will be more reason in this than in the laugh which greets him who returns from above out of the light into the cave.

[**Glaucon**] That, he said, is a very just distinction.

[**Socrates**] But then, if I am right, certain professors of education must be wrong when they say that they can put a knowledge into the soul which was not there before, like sight into blind eyes.

[**Glaucon**] They undoubtedly say this, he replied.

[**Socrates**] Whereas, our argument shows that the power and capacity of learning exists in the soul already; and that just as the eye was unable to turn from darkness to light without the whole body, so too the instrument of knowledge can only by the movement of the whole soul be turned from the world of becoming into that of being, and learn by degrees to endure the sight of being, and of the brightest and best of being, or in other words, of the good.

[**Glaucon**] Very true.

[**Socrates**] And must there not be some art which will effect conversion in the easiest and quickest manner; not implanting the faculty of sight, for that exists already, but has been turned in the wrong direction, and is looking away from the truth?

[**Glaucon**] Yes, he said, such an art may be presumed.

[**Socrates**] And whereas the other so-called virtues of the soul seem to be akin to bodily qualities, for even when they are not originally innate they can be implanted later by habit and exercise, the of wisdom more than anything else contains a divine element which always remains, and by this conversion is rendered useful and profitable; or, on the other hand, hurtful and useless. Did you never observe the narrow intelligence flashing from the keen eye of a clever rogue—how eager he is, how clearly his paltry soul sees the way to his end; he is the reverse of blind, but his keen eyesight is forced into the service of evil, and he is mischievous in proportion to his cleverness.

[**Glaucon**] Very true, he said.

[**Socrates**] But what if there had been a circumcision of such natures in the days of their youth; and they had been severed from those sensual pleasures, such as eating and drinking, which, like leaden weights, were attached to them at their birth, and which drag them down and turn the vision of their souls upon the things that are below—if, I say, they had been released from these impediments and turned in the opposite direction, the very same faculty in them would have seen the truth as keenly as they see what their eyes are turned to now.

[**Glaucon**] Very likely.

[**Socrates**] Yes, I said; and there is another thing which is likely. or rather a necessary inference from what has preceded, that neither the uneducated and uninformed of the truth, nor yet those who never make an end of their education, will be able ministers of State; not the former, because they have no single aim of duty which is the rule of all their actions, private as well as public; nor the latter, because they will not act at all except upon compulsion, fancying that they are already dwelling apart in the islands of the blest.

[**Glaucon**] Very true, he replied.

[**Socrates**] Then, I said, the business of us who are the founders of the State will be to compel the best minds to attain that knowledge which we have already shown to be the greatest of all-they must continue to ascend until they arrive at the good; but when they have ascended and seen enough we must not allow them to do as they do now.

[**Glaucon**] What do you mean?

[**Socrates**] I mean that they remain in the upper world: but this must not be allowed; they must be made to descend again among the prisoners in the cave, and partake of their labors and honors, whether they are worth having or not.

[**Glaucon**] But is not this unjust? he said; ought we to give them a worse life, when they might have a better?

[**Socrates**] You have again forgotten, my friend, I said, the intention of the legislator, who did not aim at making any one class in the State happy above the rest; the happiness was to be in the whole State, and he held the citizens together by persuasion and necessity, making them benefactors of the State, and therefore benefactors of one another; to this end he created them, not to please themselves, but to be his instruments in binding up the State.

[**Glaucon**] True, he said, I had forgotten.

[**Socrates**] Observe, Glaucon, that there will be no injustice in compelling our philosophers to have a care and providence of others; we shall explain to them that in other States, men of their class are not obliged to share in the toils of politics: and this is reasonable, for they grow up at their own sweet will, and the government would rather not have them. Being self-taught, they cannot be expected to show any gratitude for a culture which they have never received. But we have brought you into the world to be rulers of the hive, kings of yourselves and of the other citizens, and have educated you far better and more perfectly than they have been educated, and you are better able to share in the double duty. Wherefore each of you, when his turn comes, must go down to the general underground abode, and get the habit of seeing in the dark. When you have acquired the habit, you will see ten thousand times better than the inhabitants of the cave, and you will know what the several images are, and what they represent, because you have seen the beautiful and just and good in their truth. And thus our State which is also yours will be a reality, and not a dream only, and will be administered in a spirit unlike that of other States, in which men fight with one another about shadows only and are distracted in the struggle for power, which in their eyes is a great good. Whereas the truth is that the State in which the rulers are most reluctant to govern is always the best and most quietly governed, and the State in which they are most eager, the worst.

[**Glaucon**] Quite true, he replied.

[**Socrates**] And will our pupils, when they hear this, refuse to take their turn at the toils of State, when they are allowed to spend the greater part of their time with one another in the heavenly light?

[**Glaucon**] Impossible, he answered; for they are just men, and the commands which we impose upon them are just; there can be no doubt that every one of them will take office as a stern necessity, and not after the fashion of our present rulers of State.

[**Socrates**] Yes, my friend, I said; and there lies the point. You must contrive for your future rulers another and a better life than that of a ruler, and then you may have a well-ordered State; for only in the State which offers this, will they rule who are truly rich, not in silver and gold, but in virtue and wisdom, which are the true blessings of life. Whereas if they go to the administration of public affairs, poor and hungering after the' own private advantage, thinking that hence they are to snatch the chief good, order there can never be; for they will be fighting about office, and the civil and domestic broils which thus arise will be the ruin of the rulers themselves and of the whole State.

[**Glaucon**] Most true, he replied.

[**Socrates**] And the only life which looks down upon the life of political ambition is that of true philosophy. Do you know of any other?

[**Glaucon**] Indeed, I do not, he said.

[**Socrates**] And those who govern ought not to be lovers of the task? For, if they are, there will be rival lovers, and they will fight.

[**Glaucon**] No question.

[**Socrates**] Who then are those whom we shall compel to be guardians? Surely they will be the men who are wisest about affairs of State, and by whom the State is best administered, and who at the same time have other honors and another and a better life than that of politics?

[**Glaucon**] They are the men, and I will choose them, he replied.

[**Socrates**] And now shall we consider in what way such guardians will be produced, and how they are to be brought from darkness to light,—as some are said to have ascended from the world below to the gods?

[**Glaucon**] By all means, he replied.

[**Socrates**] The process, I said, is not the turning over of an oyster-shell, but the turning round of a soul passing from a day which is little better than night to the true day of being, that is, the ascent from below, which we affirm to be true philosophy?

[**Glaucon**] Quite so.

Declaration of Independence

IN CONGRESS, JULY 4, 1776

The unanimous Declaration of the thirteen United States of America

hen in the Course of human events it becomes necessary for one people to dissolve the political bands which have connected them with another and to assume among the powers of the earth, the separate and equal station to which the Laws of Nature and of Nature's God entitle them, a decent respect to the opinions of mankind requires that they should declare the causes which impel them to the separation.

We hold these truths to be self-evident, that all men are created equal, that they are endowed by their Creator with certain unalienable Rights, that among these are Life, Liberty and the pursuit of Happiness.—That to secure these rights, Governments are instituted among Men, deriving their just powers from the consent of the governed,—That whenever any Form of Government becomes destructive of these ends, it is the Right of the People to alter or to abolish it, and to institute new Government, laying its foundation on such principles and organizing its powers in such form, as to them shall seem most likely to effect their Safety and Happiness. Prudence, indeed, will dictate that Governments long established should not be changed for light and transient causes; and accordingly all experience hath shewn that mankind are more disposed to suffer, while evils are sufferable than to right themselves by abolishing the forms to which they are accustomed. But when a long train of abuses and usurpations, pursuing invariably the same Object evinces a design to reduce them under absolute Despotism, it is their right, it is their duty, to throw off such Government, and to provide new Guards for their future security.—Such has been the patient sufferance of these Colonies; and such is now the necessity which constrains them to alter their former Systems of Government. The history of the present King of Great Britain is a history of repeated injuries and usurpations, all having in direct object the establishment of an absolute Tyranny over these States. To prove this, let Facts be submitted to a candid world.

He has refused his Assent to Laws, the most wholesome and necessary for the public good.

He has forbidden his Governors to pass Laws of immediate and pressing importance, unless suspended in their operation till his Assent should be obtained; and when so suspended, he has utterly neglected to attend to them.

He has refused to pass other Laws for the accommodation of large districts of people, unless those people would relinquish the right of Representation in the Legislature, a right inestimable to them and formidable to tyrants only.

He has called together legislative bodies at places unusual, uncomfortable, and distant from the depository of their Public Records, for the sole purpose of fatiguing them into compliance with his measures.

He has dissolved Representative Houses repeatedly, for opposing with manly firmness his invasions on the rights of the people.

He has refused for a long time, after such dissolutions, to cause others to be elected, whereby the Legislative Powers, incapable of Annihilation, have returned to the People at large for their exercise; the State remaining in the mean time exposed to all the dangers of invasion from without, and convulsions within.

He has endeavoured to prevent the population of these States; for that purpose obstructing the Laws for Naturalization of Foreigners; refusing to pass others to encourage their migrations hither, and raising the conditions of new Appropriations of Lands.

He has obstructed the Administration of Justice by refusing his Assent to Laws for establishing Judiciary Powers.

He has made Judges dependent on his Will alone for the tenure of their offices, and the amount and payment of their salaries.

He has erected a multitude of New Offices, and sent hither swarms of Officers to harass our people and eat out their substance.

He has kept among us, in times of peace, Standing Armies without the Consent of our legislatures.

He has affected to render the Military independent of and superior to the Civil Power.

He has combined with others to subject us to a jurisdiction foreign to our constitution, and unacknowledged by our laws; giving his Assent to their Acts of pretended Legislation:

For quartering large bodies of armed troops among us:

For protecting them, by a mock Trial from punishment for any Murders which they should commit on the Inhabitants of these States:

For cutting off our Trade with all parts of the world:

For imposing Taxes on us without our Consent:

For depriving us in many cases, of the benefit of Trial by Jury:

For transporting us beyond Seas to be tried for pretended offences:

For abolishing the free System of English Laws in a neighbouring Province, establishing therein an Arbitrary government, and enlarging its Boundaries so as to render it at once an example and fit instrument for introducing the same absolute rule into these Colonies

For taking away our Charters, abolishing our most valuable Laws and altering fundamentally the Forms of our Governments:

For suspending our own Legislatures, and declaring themselves invested with power to legislate for us in all cases whatsoever.

He has abdicated Government here, by declaring us out of his Protection and waging War against us.

He has plundered our seas, ravaged our coasts, burnt our towns, and destroyed the lives of our people.

He is at this time transporting large Armies of foreign Mercenaries to compleat the works of death, desolation, and tyranny, already begun with circumstances of Cruelty & Perfidy scarcely paralleled in the most barbarous ages, and totally unworthy the Head of a civilized nation.

He has constrained our fellow Citizens taken Captive on the high Seas to bear Arms against their Country, to become the executioners of their friends and Brethren, or to fall themselves by their Hands.

He has excited domestic insurrections amongst us, and has endeavoured to bring on the inhabitants of our frontiers, the merciless Indian Savages whose known rule of warfare, is an undistinguished destruction of all ages, sexes and conditions.

In every stage of these Oppressions We have Petitioned for Redress in the most humble terms: Our repeated Petitions have been answered only by repeated injury. A Prince, whose character is thus marked by every act which may define a Tyrant, is unfit to be the ruler of a free people.

Nor have We been wanting in attentions to our British brethren. We have warned them from time to time of attempts by their legislature to extend an unwarrantable jurisdiction over us. We have reminded them of the circumstances of our emigration and settlement here. We have appealed to their native justice and magnanimity, and we have conjured them by the ties of our common kindred to disavow these usurpations, which would inevitably interrupt our connections and correspondence. They too have been deaf to the voice of justice and of consanguinity. We must, therefore, acquiesce in the necessity, which denounces our Separation, and hold them, as we hold the rest of mankind, Enemies in War, in Peace Friends.

We, therefore, the Representatives of the united States of America, in General Congress, Assembled, appealing to the Supreme Judge of the world for the rectitude of our intentions, do, in the Name, and by Authority of the good People of these Colonies, solemnly publish and declare, That these united Colonies are, and of Right ought to be Free and Independent States, that they are Absolved from all Allegiance to the British Crown, and that all political connection between them and the State of Great Britain, is and ought to be totally dissolved; and that as Free and Independent States, they have full Power to levy War, conclude Peace, contract Alliances, establish Commerce, and to do all other Acts and Things which Independent States may of right do.—And for the support of this Declaration, with a firm reliance on the protection of Divine Providence, we mutually pledge to each other our Lives, our Fortunes, and our sacred Honor.

—John Hancock

Fragmented by Andrei Popov

Lack of communication is an ironic result of our new and improved, high-tech communication. Why is this? Is 24-7 really good for us? What does it cost us to have more variety, more choices? Well, we get more advertising, right? Television, especially news and human interest programming is a business interest rather than a servant of a public interest. The telephone is used to buy things and connect quickly and sporadically rather than to develop real communication. The internet likewise promotes commercial, not common public interests or any sort of intelligent connection between human beings trying to better their minds, enlighten one another so as to truly help the species somehow avoid terrible mistakes. Today it's all "Move along . . . move along . . . move along." Reminds me of the way we can no longer linger while dropping off a passenger at the airport. Sure, it's not always like this. I get that. If you get to SFO at 4am you may have time for a *real* hug *outside* of the car.

One way that our ideas and conversations are fragmented occurs when we comment on a website broadcast of a news story. Most people do not actually "converse" but rather post their knee-jerk reactions, their visceral feelings; they do not read other posts and proceed to develop a conversation. It's boisterous, bombastic, bellicose and people sometimes go ballistic: "Ur so naïve. All u neocons are living in dream world" says hypertyper124." "U would say that, u dum dem [insert misspelled expletive of your choice here]. Why doncha try using your brains for a change?"

I don't think much real "brain" work is going to ensue from this exchange. But, u never no!

Discussion boards evidence the same phenomenon. Is this due to people's desires to merely emote rather than think something over? To merely agree or complain takes very little thought, little time, although some might add two or three sentences to their "I totally agree" comments: "I totally agree. U have really hit the nail on the head. Good for u!!"

How much extra time does it take to type the word *you*?

In the case where people just post a comment that is primarily expressive and then do not return to read and reply, we can see they do not really want to have a "discussion" of any length or depth. They want to complain for 10–15 seconds, hit enter, click on the next photo or link, agree for 5 seconds, hit enter and move along. Is this, by the way, good for advertisers? You betcha!

The social media and discussion boards can be used effectively to enlighten and *then* rally people to become more informed and *then* become actively engaged in issues or in conflicts, but this is not the usual way of things. As a matter of fact, some of you inwardly *replied* to that last sentence with "Oh, no. Who has the time to do all that?" or "How borrring!!!" This could be something to *discuss:* Do online thinking/reading habits actually lead to boredom and if that is so does that inure to the benefit of advertisers and the businesses they promote?

The way people post comments, without following up and conversing is tantamount to bathroom wall scribbling. Who returns to the same bathroom stall to see who has recently corresponded to their message? I can now imagine the reply I would get to that analogy if this were to be published online. Of course, few people reading online would have arrived at this fourth paragraph, having moved on after the first three sentences.

Then there are online "news" stories. They are typically in paragraphs of three to four short sentences, maybe five or six paragraphs long. No development of any single fact or event. Little if any depth or detail. Paragraphs like the one you are reading now, which is five sentences and repeats, pretty much, the same idea.

I wonder how other media affect our thinking. Television used to have programs that played the story for at least twenty minutes before commercial interruption. Now it is what, five minutes program to two minutes commercial? News stories used to last for a whole minute or two. Now it's "A terrible earthquake hit Nepal today. Over a thousand people are believed dead. The earthquake measured 7.2 on the Richter scale. In other news, Kim Kardashian has filed a law suit. . . . " At the end of an hour watching a television program, how much do we really care about or learn? Someone should conduct an experiment, have people watch 50 hours of randomly chosen television programs. These should include twenty-five hours from fifty years ago, including the news and a few movies and other entertainment vehicles (the *Jetsons*, the *Twilight Zone*, things like that) and twenty-five hours of today's T.V., including the news, which constantly shifts from one unrelated story to the next, then moves on to a two-minute commercial—"Huh? Hey, wait. What was I just thinking? Oh, look. Lowe's is having a sale!—and television sit coms that show at best one minute of one group's storyline before moving along to another story that plays for another minute then maybe cuts back to the other for a minute before a commercial. Here we have Jose and Samantha (aka Sammy) going to visit her mother to discuss buying an iPhone. Mother is resistant, but the kids are determined to better her quality of life. Queue music. Now we are in Ireland where Brian and Stephen have travelled to be gay married. Brian loses his wallet and . . . " What is going on here? Who knows? Who cares? I forgot already . . .

Yes, there are television programs here in the U.S. that are not constantly interrupted. Yes, there are places on the internet where we can find news reports that provide us with significant details and meaningful insights. Yes, there are sites on the internet that further real learning . . . but . . . I just went to check the spelling of *travelled*. Having studied mostly English rather than American literature, I tend to spell it with two ll's. After clicking on the Oxford English Dictionary website's English button, a lady popped up saying "It's free. Try it now." r u kidding?

Distracted: The New News World and the Fate of Attention by Maggie Jackson

Last summer, I was a passenger in a car barreling down a Detroit highway when I noticed a driver speeding past us, a magazine propped up beside his steering wheel. Perhaps most amazingly, I was the only person in my group who was surprised by this high-speed feat of multitasking.

Today, it's rare to give anything our full attention. Our focus is fragmented and diffused, whether we're conversing, eating, working, minding our kids—or imbibing the news. A new hypermobile, cybercentric and split-focused world has radically changed the context of news consumption—and shifted the environment for newsgathering as well. Attention is the bedrock of deep learning, critical thinking, and creativity—all skills that we need to foster, not undercut, more than ever on both sides of the newsmaking fence. And as we become more culturally attention-deficient, I worry about whether we as a nation can nurture both an informed citizenry—and an informative press.

It's easy to point first to rising data floods as a culprit for our distraction. More than 100 million blogs and a like number of Web sites, not to mention 1.8 million books in print, spawn so much information that, as Daniel Boorstin observes, data begin to outstrip the making of meaning. "We are captives of information," writes the cultural historian Walter Ong, "for uninterrupted information can create an information chaos and, indeed, has done so, and quite clearly will always do so."

Yet sense-making in today's information-rich world is not just a matter of how much we have to contend with but, more importantly, how we approach the 24/7 newsfeed that is life today. Consider the Detroit driver; where was he consuming media, and how much focus was he allotting to the task?

Increasingly, Americans are on the go, whatever they're doing. Just 14 percent of us move each year, yet the average number of miles that we drive annually has risen 80 percent during the past two decades. The car-as-moving-den, the popularity of power bars and other portable cuisine, the rise of injuries related to "textwalking," all of these—and more—attest to our collective hyperactivity. And as we relentlessly hurry through our days toting hand-held foods and portable gadgets, at the same time we keep one ear or eye on multiple streams of news-bytes.

Fragmented Attention

As a term, "multitasking" doesn't quite do justice to all the ways in which we fragment our attention. Split-focus is sometimes simply the result of living in a highly mediated world. More than half of children ages eight to 18 live in homes where a television is on most of the time, an environment linked to attention difficulties and lowered parent-child interaction. In public spaces from elevators to taxis, screens packed with flickering words and images are increasingly hard to avoid. Despite reconnaissance forays up and down airports, I usually have to succumb to an inescapable TV blare while waiting to fly. Former Microsoft executive Linda Stone deems ours a landscape of "continuous partial attention." Tuning in and out is a way of life.

But split focus also occurs when we hopscotch from one task or person to another, as most famously exemplified by the lethal crash of a California commuter train, apparently because the rail engineer at the helm was texting. Our veneration of multitasking can be traced in part to the influential efficiency guru Frederick W. Taylor, who counseled that factory work could be speeded up if broken down into interchangeable parts. As well, we live in an era where we seem to believe that we can shape time at will. We ignore age-old rhythms of sun and season, strain to surpass our biological limitations, and now seek to break the fetters of mechanized time by trying to do two or more things at once. Multitasking is born of a post-clock era.

The result on the job is "work fragmentation," according to Gloria Mark, an informatics professor at the University of California, Irvine and a leader in the field of "interruption science." In studies across a range of industries, she and other researchers have found that office workers change tasks on average every three minutes throughout the day. An e-mail, instant message, phone call, colleague's question, or a new thought prompts an interruption. Once interrupted, it takes nearly 25 minutes to return to an original task. Half of the time, people are interrupting themselves.

The risks are clear. "If you're continually interrupted and switching thoughts, it's hard to think deeply about anything," Mark once observed to me. "How can you engage with something?"

In our rapid-fire, split-focus era, are we able to process, filter and reflect well on the tsunamis of information barraging us daily? Are we hearing, but not listening? If this continues to be the way we work, learn and report, could we be collectively nurturing new forms of ignorance, born not from a dearth of information as in the past, but from an inability or an unwillingness to do the difficult work of forging knowledge from the data flooding our world?

I see worrisome signs that our climate of distraction undermines our ability to think deeply. Consider that nearly a third of workers are so busy or interrupted that they often feel they do not have time to reflect on the work that they do, according to the Families and Work Institute. David M. Levy, a professor at the University of Washington, has even held a high-level MacArthur Foundation-funded conference tellingly called, "No Time to Think." And for all their tech-fluency, younger generations often have trouble evaluating and assessing information drawn from the Web, studies show. For example, a new national exam of information literacy, the Educational Testing Service's "iSkills" assessment test, found that just half of college students could judge the objectivity of a Web site, and just over a third could correctly narrow an overly broad online search.

Multitasking and the News

News consumption fares no better, according to a small but in-depth recent study of 18- to 34-year-olds commissioned by The Associated Press. The 18 participants, who were tracked by ethnographers for days, consumed a "steady diet of bite-size pieces of news," almost always while multitasking. Their news consumption was often "shallow and erratic," even as they yearned to go beyond the brief and often repetitive headlines and updates that barraged them daily. Participants "appeared debilitated by information overload and unsatisfying news experiences," researchers observed. Moreover, "when the news wore them down, participants in the study showed a tendency to passively receive versus actively seek news."

This is a disturbing portrait: multitasking consumers uneasily "snacking" on headlines, stuck on the surface of the news, unable to turn information into knowledge.

Are consumers lazy? Are the media to blame? Or is Google making us stupid, as a recent Atlantic magazine cover story asked? It's far too simplistic to look for a single culprit, a clear-cut driver of such changes. Rather, helped by influential tools that are seedbeds of societal change, we've built a culture over generations that prizes frenetic movement, fragmented work, and instant answers. Just today, my morning paper carried a front-page story about efforts "in a new age of impatience" to create a quick-boot computer. Explained one tech executive, "It's ridiculous to ask people to wait a couple of minutes" to start up their computer. The first hand up in the classroom, the hyper-businessman who can't sit still, much less listen—these are markers of success in American society.

Of course, the news business has always been quick, fast and fueled by multitasking. Reporters work in one of the most distracting of milieus—and yet draw on reserves of just-in-time focus to meet deadlines. Still, perhaps today we need to consider how much we can shrink editorial attention spans, with our growing emphasis on "4D" newsgathering, Twitter-style reporting, and newsfeeds from citizen bloggers whose influence far outstrips any hard-won knowledge of the difficult craft of journalism. It's not just news consumers who are succumbing to a dangerous dependence on what's first up on Google for making sense of their world.

Ultimately, our new world does more than speed life up and pare the news down. Most importantly, our current climate undermines the trio of skills—focus, awareness and planning/judgment—that make up the crucial human faculty of attention. When we split our focus, curb our awareness, and undercut our ability to gain perspective, we diminish our ability to think critically, carry out deep learning, or be creative. Can we afford to create an attention-deficit economy or press, or build a healthy democracy from a culture of distraction? Absolutely not.

Maggie Jackson is the author of "Distracted: The Erosion of Attention and the Coming Dark Age," published by Prometheus Books in June 2008. She writes the "Balancing Acts" column in The Boston Globe, and her work has appeared in The New York Times, BusinessWeek and on NPR, among other national publications.

Despicable Us: Scott Walker, the Media and the 2016 Presidential Campaign by Frank Bruni

Maybe those of us who write about politics and campaigns should adopt a bristly uniform of hair shirts, so that we're constantly atoning for our sins.

Maybe we should wear targets, the better for our critics to take aim at us.

Oh, how we're hated. And as another presidential race takes shape, that hatred gathers force. Hillary Clinton's protectors cast us as bloodthirsty raptors intent on finding flaw where none exists. Chris Christie was asked what he'd given up for Lent and said it would have been *The New York Times*, but then his priest told him he had to forswear something he'd truly miss.

Scott Walker thinks we're laying an elaborate trap for him, and after *The Washington Post* inquired if he regarded President Obama as Christian, he not only punted but also bellowed about "gotcha" questions, griping: "This is a classic example of why people hate Washington and, increasingly, they dislike the press."

Dislike? Increasingly? Either he was being charitable or he hasn't read the polling. The public's esteem for us has been abysmal for a good long while.

And if we're honest, we've brought much of it on ourselves. We play petty games and barrel down pointless roads.

There are bad habits we should surrender not merely for Lent but forever, and there are tweaks we'd be wise to implement as we move forward with the 2016 election.

Here's a wish list of such amendments, followed by a look at what we do right, because there's plenty of that as well. I hasten to add that I have been guilty of all the high crimes and misdemeanors I describe.

Stop hyping Iowa and New Hampshire. You would think, from our rapt (and sometimes rabid) attention to Iowa caucuses and the New Hampshire primary, that candidates face some sort of mathematical, structural imperative to wow voters there, and that these two states are nonpareil mirrors of the country.

Hardly. The importance of the contests stems chiefly from our coverage of them; the momentum that winners and runners-up carry out of them is as much our decree as it is anything organic.

Iowa is not America, just one rectangular slice of it. It's about twice as rural as the rest of the nation, more religiously conservative and much less Hispanic and black.

In 2012, when Rick Santorum prevailed in the Republican caucuses there, only 121,501 voters participated. That was less than one in five registered Republicans in the state.

Of those 121,501 voters, 57 percent described themselves as born-again or evangelical Christians, according to the Pew Research Center. That's wholly out of whack with the concentration of such religious conservatives in the party nationally, as a recent column I wrote about new data from the Public Religion Research Institute made clear.

Go easy on the spouses. There's a rickety logic behind our spirited plunge into the psyches, hobbies and wardrobes of candidates' other halves, and there's a sexist, gratuitously invasive edge to it.

Yes, the marriage choice that a person makes is profoundly reflective of his or her character, but it's typically made at a young age. People change, as do marriages.

And the idea that a spouse is a full-fledged, fully involved political partner whose priorities will color a presidential administration is highly questionable, the Clintons excepted. Laura Bush's policy imprint on George fell somewhere between marginal and invisible.

Outside the political arena, the marriage of a person who is up for a big job isn't considered some special window or yardstick. I'm hard pressed to think of business titans and corporate C.E.O.s who are judged by their spouses, and those spouses draw limited scrutiny. Let's take a bit of a cue from that.

Don't buy tickets to circus acts. When someone on the fringes of both the race and serious discourse says something clownish that's a cry to be noticed, ignore it. This means quitting our addiction to Donald Trump, Sarah Palin and Rudy Giuliani, no matter how good they are for readership, ratings and belly laughs.

We are too often like the parents who attend only to the screeching 3-year-old, plying him with Gummi bears and Goldfish crackers, which simply reward and ratchet up his screams. Meanwhile the virtuous, unexcitable older sibling is ignored, until she wins the Michigan primary and leaves us no choice but a grudging belated magazine cover.

Resist glorifying certain horses for the sake of having a horse race. Some are obviously bound, in the end, for the political glue factory. Remember Michele Bachmann and Herman Cain in 2012? Enough said.

Resist declaring emergencies where they don't exist. We may wish certain snags were roadblocks and certain missteps collapses, because we think they should be or they're sexier that way. But we look foolish when we're wrong. After Walker's supposed bungling of the Obama-Christian question, he went up in one national poll.

Sometimes a dodge is just a dodge and a gaffe not much of a gaffe. The world keeps spinning; the campaign trundles on.

Resist overly tidy diagnoses of the nation's mood. Four people drinking coffee on a street corner of Hardscrabble, Del., or Ordinary, Va., do not constitute a snapshot of the electorate, no matter how fetching their town's name.

We err when we suggest otherwise.

But we have our strengths.

Over the last decade, there's been something of a surge in the truth-squad vetting of the insults that candidates hurl and the claims that they make: on the trail, in debates, at conventions. It's exemplified by such popular, praiseworthy sites and writers as PolitiFact and *The Washington Post*'s Glenn Kessler, whose

Fact Checker column doles out Pinocchios in accordance with the size of the politician's lie. This is a vital task.

The widely derided "process" stories that we do on the agility or clumsiness with which a candidate's campaign unfurls also matter, as do the introductions we give voters to a candidate's aides. These provide a predictive glimpse of the candidate as chief executive of a sprawling, unpredictable enterprise, which is what the president of the United States is.

A president is also someone whose every word, scripted or spontaneous, is heard loudly and can have great consequence, and so most of our supposed "gotcha" questions are anything but. They're part of a rolling, roiling back-and-forth that tells voters essential truths about a politician's capabilities under a constant spotlight like the presidency's.

Keep that in mind when candidates bemoan and disparage the media's omnipresence and hypervigilance, and remember this, too: When they're harping about our shortcomings, they're first and foremost trying to cover up their own.

I invite you to follow me on Twitter at twitter.com/frankbruni and join me on Facebook.

APPENDIX I

Recommended Texts and Videos

If you found fallacy identification fascinating, check out the following texts and videos and see if you can find some more.

1. *Inherit the Wind*

   This film contains premises, fallacies, causal argument, and indeed, all of the elements of argument (thesis, counterargument, refutation, concession).

   I recommend the older version with Spencer Tracy. The new one is okay, but the fallacies and premises are a little less obvious. It seems to be a nicer version, and that's not helpful to you.

2. *Judgment Day.*

   Online video. Church vs. State. Creationism, under the guise of intelligent design vs evolution; a court case documentary approx 1.15 hrs

   Analyze evidence (testimonial, scientific, physical evidence) and fallacies, esp. equivocation. What is the question at issue?
   http://video.pbs.org/video/980040807/

3. *12 Angry Men*

   Either version will do. Many clearly stated, unacceptable premises at the beginning, and a whole smorgasbord of fallacies. Also contains elements of the arguments listed under *Inherit the Wind.*

4. *Harrison Bergeron*

   This film may be a little difficult to find. It's based on a short story by Kurt Vonnegut. The question at issue here is, "How much equality do we really want?"

   It is very enjoyable and really stimulates critical thinking. It is rated R, but I don't know why.

5. Plato's *Euthyphro and Crito.*

Available online or in bookstores. Helpful for analyzing objective observation, symbolism, and hypothetical reasoning.

6. *Crash*. 2004 film directed by Paul Haggis. Prejudice in LA runs amuck but eventually enlightenment is found after careful directing!

7. Orwell's *1984*.

Writing and Formatting Critical Thinking Papers: Causal and Argument Essays/MLA

How to Write a Cause/Effect Argument Essay

One must take several steps to research, write, and then document a causal argument essay.

Step one: Decide on your topic. If you have been asked to argue, you will need to as well write out your thesis in a way such that reasonable people could disagree with you. Work on that. Figure out first, what is your question at issue.

Consider Supports: Choose from one of several disciplines, e.g., medicine, law, economics, history, social sciences (anthropology, psychology, sociology) for support. You should be looking for articles that have a clear *thesis* and *premises* that are acceptable. As well, you should find some article that will contain the *counterargument*, an opponent's view. You will argue that his/her *premise* is unacceptable or that his thesis is flawed, or you may argue that the steps in his/her inductive logic are somehow flawed. Perhaps this person has failed to consider something important, or has missed a step or two because he/she has come to the conclusion too hastily. You should also be on the lookout for an article that *refutes* the opposition, one that supports your *assertions*. You will need to include a *refutation* in your argument.

Step two: Narrow your focus. Start by looking for a news story from a newspaper, magazine article, or television, or perhaps from a history lesson. Research this via the newspaper websites or look through one of the hundreds of magazines on your library's magazine racks. Sometimes just a headline can pique your curiosity. You can also try to recall some history lesson, either from school or the History Channel (info for which is also available at Historychannel.com) that caused you to wonder "why?" You can also check the archived videos on pbs.org or C-SPAN.

For example, what caused the children of Germany to buy into Hitler's youth program? On the other hand, if you would like to research scientific stories, you can go to websites such as Discovery-channel.com or even pbs.org or pick up a copy of *Scientific American*. Sometimes network stations also run stories on scientific causal arguments. MSNBC, ABC, and CBS include investigative, research-type stories on their web pages, some scientific or medical arguments currently under debate. For medical terminology and explanations as well as articles, you could go to WebMD.com. Besides this, there is C-SPAN. C-SPAN.org gives you access to many political, legal, and social arguments. For background facts, you can access Factsonfile.com. Finally, you can go to the library and research recent newspaper articles using the ProQuest software. Make sure to write down all of the information you will need for your footnotes, endnotes, or works cited page. Use EasyBib (www.EasyBib.org) to keep track of your sources. Use the owl/pur-due website to construct your APA References or your MLA Works Cited.

When citing websites, keep track of both dates, if applicable, i.e., the date of original publication and the date you viewed the website. Also, make sure there is an author. Most teachers will not accept a website reference without an author. I won't.

Step three: After you select an article that contains a causal argument or implication of an argument, research the evidence presented in the article. If someone says that the Hitler youth were influenced easily because kids are inclined to want to please their elders and believe them, find some psychologist, someone in the field who specifically speaks to the "influences on children" issue, to back up this *infer-ence,* the conclusion drawn from evidence.

Step four: Try to find someone who disagrees with the cause your source implies. This is known as *refutation.* The author should have ethos appeal (good reputation) for the purpose of your paper. If it is a sci-ence paper, don't pick a politician, in other words. Don't choose an editorial, either, or a blog. Stick with publications from journals or scholarly works.

Give two statements by this authority that show his/her rebuttal to the first article or news show's assertion.

Step five: Looking over both arguments, try to find validity and logic in each. Think about what concession you could make to the opponent's argument. A *concession* is when you give your opponent a point. For example, you might say, "Mr. X has a point. There is no real way to be sure that some other outside force was not at work."

Step six: Write your rough draft. Begin by introducing your source, your primary source, and continue by stating clearly why the causal argument he/she puts forward is credible. Don't go into detail yet. Then acknowledge there is some refutation. Finish the introduction by saying what the *question at issue* seems to be, and whether the research you did backed up the argument presented in the original source.

The body paragraphs should consist of both author's arguments briefly summarized, then analyzed, and your objective, logical consideration of the validity of his/her points. Include:

1. Author's premise (Mr. X says that the youth did this because children are . . .). If the premise is unstated, explain what he must believe in order to consider his assessment of the cause as valid.

2. Your consideration of this premise as acceptable or not.

3. The author's reasoning, including quotes from the author. Is he/she too narrow? Is he/she omitting information that should be considered? Are there any studies, and if so, are they valid? Discuss his/her evidence, and qualify it as either legitimate and substantial or not so.

4. Your final analysis of his/her reasoning. What impression are you left with? Are you convinced?

5. A final consideration of some opponent's position/premises/supports.

Conclude by offering:

1. Your evaluation of both arguments.

2. Your ideas as to how the argument(s) could be improved or perhaps just updated. Is there new evidence out there, or new technology that could have made a difference in their perspectives, yet it has been overlooked?

3. What do you think are the primary causes left to be investigated.

4. A suggestion that some other contributing factor should be considered. What follows is a set of guidelines for writing an MLA-style paper. For more formatting information, MLA or APA, see the owl/purdue website.

Summarizing, Analyzing and Evaluating (SAE)

Why write a summary? Write a summary when you wish to ensure that you really understand something that you read or when you need to provide some *essential* background so that the reader will have necessary context. The word essential has two meanings here. Essential means only what is needed for your reader to have a basic understanding of the text and essential also means that you leave out the details or any fluff (see Chapter One of *Making Sense*: Language Fluffery).

When should you write a summary? Write the summary as you *actively read* the work the second time or even the third time. If you are reading a long work, like a novel, write short summaries of chapters after you annotate and then take notes (in a journal, preferably). You can use the notes and annotations to help you analyze later on, too. If you are reading an article or an argument, include only the essential information: name of the work, type of work (story, article, essay, etc.), author's name, when and where it was published, thesis, supports and evidence. Stay away from online summaries; they tend to be subjective. Don't include any editorial comment that prefaces an article or story, introductory material that we find in anthologies sometimes. These are paragraphs offering biographical information about the author, why she wrote the story, etc. They do not belong in *your* summary. You must summarize just the work itself and do it on your own. Here's how.

Summarizing

- Begin the summary with a reference to the writer (full name the first time you cite him/her and after that, last name with any title like Professor, Doctor, etc.); the title of the article; the thesis, in your own words. Example: Psychologist Carl Rogers, in his article "Communication: Its Blocking and Facilitation," enlightens us regarding certain methods therapists can employ in order to avoid communication barriers. According to Rogers, [thesis in your own words goes here]."
- Write in a direct, objective style, using your own words. Avoid verbs like seems, and subjective adjectives such as many, very, quite (See Ch. 1 *Making Sense*).
- Leave out quotes.

- Include only key ideas, evidence and supports, not specific details.
- Let your reader see the connections the author makes (logical, illogical; chronological connections between events that are implied). You can note some connections that seem to be contradictory.

"Although the author mentions x in paragraph three, in the fifth paragraph he provides testimonial evidence that contrasts with . . ."

- No judging or evaluating when writing your summary.
- Leave out your personal opinion.

As you take notes, ask questions: What is the author's apparent purpose? Is he/she persuading or convincing? Is he/she mostly trying to inform or perhaps enlighten his readers? You will not be assuming that you know what the author is *trying to say*. Rather, consider the diction, thesis, evidence and type of support for their effect on you as you read. Do you feel informed, persuaded, enlightened? Determining purpose will help you choose *signal phrases* as you summarize the author's ideas.

- What are types of support that you should look for while reading? Try to annotate as you read and note.
- Examples—includes hypothetical example, personal, historical, literary, film . . .
- Comparisons (including figurative language)
- Contrast
- Cause-effect reasoning
- Evidence
- Definitions

Analyzing

Analysis is an objective, detached act. You are not taking an optimistic or a pessimistic approach but rather staying as neutral as you can be. Analysis requires that you make some observations, objective observations that take time. While you are analyzing you are engaged and reading the whole text. Engaged means you are actively looking for connections, patterns as you note the organization of the work. You are noting repeated or related words and ideas as you analyze the author's language. You are questioning the logic or the causal reasoning and thinking critically rather than making judgments or forming opinions about the issue. You are taking it apart and putting things together. This part, unlike the summary, will include some quoting. Keep the size of the quotes and number of quotes to a reasonable amount.

Use signal words to introduce your response and the quoted material. Key signal phrases you can use to avoid saying "the author talks about" a million times in your essay are below. Instead of "The author talks about" can write The author:

- advocates
- admonishes
- asserts
- contends
- elaborates on
- elicits
- elucidates
- emphasizes
- equivocates

hypothesizes
informs readers that
infers
insists
integrates
interprets
juxtaposes
laments
lashes out

maintains
opines
pontificates
posits
promotes
proposes
speculates
suggests
wonders

Evaluating

When you evaluate, you can question and analyze and note your objections to the author's reasoning, the validity of his facts or relevance of his evidence, just to list a few things that reasonable people evaluate, but you should base your evaluation on the text and your previous analysis. Personal, subjective opinions are not useful. Try to keep your evaluation *almost* professional. Be fair, considering good and not so good points.

Example student response paragraph *with summary*, analysis and evaluation

Professor Cantor asserts the premise that. . . . He basis his belief on evidence that is supplied by *Time* magazine, an article that gives costs of certain body parts charged by sellers in India. He asserts that. . . . As evidence he offers. . . . He concludes by. . . . His thesis is. . . .

This might sound reasonable, but one must ask, is his premise acceptable? Does he know anyone, or can he cite facts about. . . .? The connection that he makes between . . . and . . . suggests a causal link between. . . . The statistic that he uses as support relates to. . . .and is valid. His statistical analysis, however . . . because. . . .

His reasoning is flawed to the degree that he does not sufficiently make a connection between the ultimate effect and the cause, but the statistic does help us. . . . The authority that he has cited seems irrelevant as well because. . . . What might be more relevant to the narrowed focus he has chosen, economic reasons for changing the law, would be some evidence. . . .

APPENDIX III

MLA Essay Formatting and Incorporating Quoted Material, Parenthetical Citation & Works Cited (and avoiding plagiarism!)

MLA Format Basics

1. Spacing: MLA style research papers should be typed, double-spaced. with 1 inch margins all around.

2. Current 2012 MLA rules do NOT require a title page.

3. MLA essays require a header. Insert a header, upper right, one that contains your last name, two spaces then the page number. It should appear on each page of your esssay.

4. Title, centered, appears one double space below your heading. DO NOT BOLD, ALL CAP OR UNDERLINE THE TITLE. DON'T HYPERFONT IT. IT SHOULD JUST BE NORMAL PRINT TYPE AND SIZE. EXAMPLE:

Source: http://owl.english.purdue.edu (this site has helpful writing lessons—spelling & grammar, writing introductions & conclusions—too!)

Arthur Anderson
Professor Stevens
English 1-097
January 25, 2007

Fixing Enron

5. Indent each paragraph 5 spaces. Do not double space between paragraphs.

6. Font type Times New Roman is acceptable. Size 12 font.

7. Use quotation marks around titles of short works and italicize titles of longer works (so, short story or poem = quotation marks; novel = italics)

8. Do not address the reader as "you." Use "one" or "people," etc. instead.

9. Offset 1″ from left margin quotes that are more than four printed lines. Do not use quote marks.

10. Use parenthetical source citation rather than foot notes and be sure to introduce and qualify sources, unless the source is a well known organization or professional.

Incorporating Quoted Material, Parenthetical Citation and Works Cited

Cite Sources: All direct quotes must be cited; all ideas or facts taken from some other writer, even though in your own words, must be cited. It is PLAGIARISM if you copy another's words without quoting! If you paraphrase another's ideas or words without giving credit to the author, it is still PLAGIARISM! Your school website tells you what constitutes plagiarism. Plagiarism is using the words, specific ideas or reasoning of another without giving attribution. To avoid even the possibility that you are plagiarizing, give attribution (credit) to your source.

"According to Professor Stevens in her lovely book *Making Sense: A guide to sound reasoning and critical thinking* which is now in its marvelous 5th edition because, again according to Professor Stevens, 'Plagiarism is not unavoidable.' Clearly she holds the premise that plagiarism can be controlled."

Always follow up a quote with a comment. Here is a pattern to follow until you become familiar with this practice: Comment—quote—comment. . . . (CQC).

You can comment or ask a question. Use signal phrases that are relevant to your purpose for including quoted material and always identify your source first, give the reader some idea why he/she/they are reputable, credible, relevant, or authoritative.

Use a pair of commas to insert author info; this is an "appositional" reference. Use signal phrases, listed below.

Ex: Andre Popov, Professor of Cultural Anthropology at the University of Minnesota, interprets the data to mean "various cultures. . . ."

Key signal phrases you can use to avoid saying "the author talks about" a million times in your essay are below. Instead of "The author talks about" you can write "The author:

• advocates	hypothesizes	maintains
• admonishes	informs readers that	opines
• asserts	interprets	pontificates
• contends	insists	proposes
• elucidates	juxtaposes	speculates
• emphasizes	laments	suggests
• equivocates	lashes out	wonders

Works Cited Page

1. All titles of works that contributed ideas and information to the paper should be listed. Indent five spaces or one-half inch after the first line of each entry.

2. Italicize titles of books, magazines, newspapers, journals, and titles of subscription databases. Enclose titles of articles, essays, poems, and short stories that are part of a source in quotations marks. Titles of government documents do not need quote marks or italics.

3. When citing Internet resources put the date you accessed the source right before the URL of the source, if your instructor requires it. [It is optional.]

4. Abbreviate the names of all months in dates except May, June, and July.

5. Be sure to alphabetize your Works Cited page by the last name of the author of the citation or the first word of the title of the citation if the author's name is not given.

6. Include all relevant information (author, title, publisher, publication date, date first published and accessed if a web source and the medium (Web, Print, DVD, etc.)

Parenthetical Documentation

1. MLA recommends parenthetical documentation instead of footnoting. Parenthetical documentation is a brief reference in the paper directly after the sentence or paragraph in which you quote from the book or use its ideas. The authors name and page number correlates with an entry on the list of authors in the Works Cited. This takes the place of a footnote. If the Works Cited lists a work by title, use a shortened form of the title and page number. Say you are writing about Carter Hardy's belief that females desire leadership less than men. Integrate the quote following your question and give the author and page number: So, do women really "rely on leaders more than men" as Carter Hardy maintains (*Leadership and Gender* 184)?

2. When the author is mentioned in the sentence only include the page number in the parentheses. Place the period after the parentheses, not within the quotation marks. For example: Carter Hardy believes that the "increased intake of sugar cereals among teachers has significantly raised classroom narcolepsy" (106).

3. When the author is not mentioned by name, put both the author's last name and the page number in the parentheses. Do not put a comma in between them. For example: "Increased intake of sugar cereals among teachers has significantly raised classroom narcolepsy" (Hardy 106).

4. When there is no author, use the first word (or first few words) of the title of the book or article (article title words in quotations). Many people lament the loss of quality television time to the imposition of family interaction ("America" 33).

5. If multiple authors: *Two authors:* "If you think about it, the human species produces more tin foil than plastic wrap" (Clinton and Bush 90). *Three authors:* (Clinton, Bush, and Reagan 99). *More than three authors:* (Clinton et al. 104.)

6. When using a quote that was already a quote in your sources: Lou Reed told us to "Take a walk on the wild side" (qtd. in Roller). In this situation, the quote by Lou Reed was found by the student as a quote in a book by Roller.

7. If your information is from a full-text article from a database or the Internet, there may be no page number. If so, use (Author n.pag.) to show that no pagination was available.

Important Information

Remember that works cited lists are alphabetized by the first word of each citation.

Ignore A, AN, or THE when alphabetizing.

Double space your Works Cited List within and between entries.

Abbreviate the names of all months in dates except May, June, and July.

Title your works cited list Works Cited and center it on the page.

Include the medium last; note the word Web below?

Example:

> Shulte, Bret. "Putting a Price on Pollution; Climate change laws seem inevitable, but their economic impact is unknown." *US News & World Report* 14 May 2007. 24 May 2007. Web.

Common Abbreviations Used in Works Cited Lists

ed. — editor, edition, edited by
eds. — editors
n.d. — no date of publication
n.p. — no publisher given
n.pag. — page numbering not available
qtd. — quoted
U — University
UP — University Press
vol. — volume
writ. — writer, written by
Jan., Feb., Mar., Apr., Aug., Sept., Oct., Nov., and Dec.

Works Cited practice test (answers on last page of Appendix III)

1. How would you cite an article titled "10 Tips on writing the Living Web" published on August 16th, 2002 by Mark Bernstein found on *A List Apart Magazine* and retrieved today, July 11, 2012?

2. How would you cite the movie, "High Fidelity"?

3. You find a recipe for vegetarian chili and want to use it in your nutrition class. How would you cite it if you found it on ehow.com July 11, 2012?

Works Cited Sample Page

The following shows a complete works cited page for a paper on aids. It includes appropriate citations for print and online encyclopedia articles, books, magazine, newspaper, and journal articles from the actual periodicals or full-text databases, videotapes, and a web site. Source: http://owl.english.purdue.edu/owl/resource/557/14/

Works Cited

"Business Coalition for Climate Action Doubles." *Environmental Defense.* 8 May 2007. Environmental Defense Organization. 24 May 2007. Web.

Clinton, Bill. Interview. *New York Times on the Web.* May 2007. 25 May 2007 Keyword: Climate. Web.

Dean, Cornelia. "Executive on a Mission: Saving the Planet." *New York Times on the Web* 22 May 2007. 25 May 2007. Web.

Ebert, Robert. "An Inconvenient Truth." Rev. of *An Inconvenient Truth,* dir. Davis Guggenheim. *rogerebert.com.* 2 June 2006. 24 May 2007. Web.

Gowdy, John. "Avoiding Self-organized Extinction: Toward a Co-evolutionary Economics of Sustainability." *International Journal of Sustainable Development and World Ecology.* 14.1 (2007): 27–36. Print.

An Inconvenient Truth. Dir. Davis Guggenheim. Perf. Al Gore. Lawrence Bender, 2006. DVD.

Leroux, Marcel. "Global Warming: Myth Or Reality?: The Erring Ways of Climatology. New York: Harcourt Brace. (2005). 23. Print.

Milken, Michael, Gary Becker, Myron Scholes, and Daniel Kahneman. "On Global Warming and Financial Imbalances." *New Perspectives Quarterly* 23.4 (2006): 63.

Nordhaus, William D. "After Kyoto: Alternative Mechanisms to Control Global Warming." *American Economic Review* 96.2 (2006): 31–34. Print.

———. "Global Warming Economics." *Science* 9 Nov. 2001: 1283–84. 24 May 2007. Print.

Shulte, Bret. "Putting a Price on Pollution; Climate change laws seem inevitable, but their economic impact is unknown." *US News & World Report* 14 May 2007. 24 May 2007. Print.

Uzawa, Hirofumi. *Economic Theory and Global Warming.* Cambridge: Cambridge UP, 2003. Print.

How to Research Efficiently and Select Qualified Supports

When required, research is serious work. It is expected that you will begin your research with a research question in mind. This is like math (solve for x) and not like just searching the internet to find something.

Never just find things and put them in your paper because they sort of relate. That you did so will be evident. (Don't underestimate the intelligence of your reader.)

Instead, begin by asking questions that relate to some aspect of the topic that you are really interested in. By doing this you accomplish two things. First, you are relating to the topic, thinking actively about it. Second, you are becoming interested as soon as you ask the question, what interests me? Review Chapter One of *Making Sense* to see what I mean by avoiding faulty assumptions. Keep your thinking objective. If you find that your list is too general, try to use specific adjectives.

Example Topic: Women's Health

Question: Why is women's health different from men's (Assuming something, there. Revise)

Question: Is women's health different from men's? (Too broad)

Question: Is women's mental health different from men's? (much better and could be even better with more refinement)

Sources

The first thing to keep in mind as a critical thinker assigned a research paper is to have a clear idea of what your narrowed topic and then tentative thesis will be before going on line or visiting the library.

Thus you can avoid randomly accumulating notes and URL's which will inevitably lead to a "randomish" paper. Do the thinking and questioning that I recommended first. Talk it over with others. How can you support your tentative thesis? What might some people object to? Have you made any faulty assumptions? What kind of evidence could you possibly find? Is there any evidence that might contradict your ideas? (If so, go ahead and look for and even include some). Where could you find relevant sources?

Figure out generally where you want to go before you head off on the road to research.

Next, you should never "assume" when it comes to sources. Ask your teacher. How old can the sources be? Is there a cut-off time to avoid outdated material or data?

The next most important consideration is how much you want to include of your thoughts and how heavily you wish to rely on outside sources. Your instructor has probably given you some idea as to this.

Finally, you should consider how you will stay organized and avoid plagiarism. Plagiarism is borrowing someone else's ideas, wording and not giving "attribution" or credit. This can result when students feel rushed and become disorganized.

Most research papers will require more than just a couple of sources. They will require facts, examples, authoritative opinions and perhaps statistics. The student should keep track of these sources and once he/she feels there is a sufficiency, organize them. The presentation of your evidence and support should logical, orderly.

Once you have some relevant, credible sources, summarize and qualify them. Question your sources. Find out who they are, what they have done.

Do this before you write your research essay.

In the case of a web page, you can usually see an About Us button. Click on that.

Some students are familiar with the abbreviations in the web address/URL which signify certain types of web pages. They see an "edu." and think, "That's an education site. This must be a legit source." Not true. Question your sources, always. Go to the About Us button on the Home Page or Google the names of any contributors to the site if you can't locate the owner of the copy write for the website. To minimize your time, rather than using Google to search, go through a university or college website. Librarians select carefully material which is relevant and valuable to college research, so the links they provide to journals and statistical sites are useful.

The University of California also has a valuable site: *http://infomine.ucr. edu/*

Observe and Analyze while Reading Sources

- Always observe the author's language and question: Is it mostly factual or mostly opinion? Is the topic developed enough or are there just a few sentences per paragraph and do the sub-topics change rapidly and/or seem only loosely related? Does the author qualify his/her "evidence" or any witnesses, authorities?
- After you get a pretty good idea how things are shaping up, go ahead and make an outline that includes the sources. Write out, just for yourself, how

the sources will fit in, why you are using them and how you will qualify them. You are responsible for avoiding plagiarism, and this is a good way to do just that. Include those parenthetical references.

- Before or while you write your rough draft, go ahead and double-check those sources. Make sure you are not using a source like the ACLU assuming it is an objective, scholarly government entity when in reality many people, including your teachers, see it as almost opposite.

- If you have questions about the legitimacy of your sources you can do two things, depending on how much time you have before your finished draft is due on your teacher's computer or her desk: (1) email your instructor or (2) Reference librarian if you are in the library.

Correct Answers to Works Cited Practice Test

1. Bernstein, Mark. "10 Tips on Writing the Living Web." *A List Apart: For People Who Make Websites*. A List Apart Mag., 16 Aug. 2002. Web. 11 July 2012.

2. *High Fidelity*. Dir. Stephen Frears. Perf. John Cusack, Iben Hjejle, Jack Black, and Todd Louiso. 2000. Walt Disney Video, 2001. DVD.

3. "How to Make Vegetarian Chili *eHow.com*, n.d. Web. 11 July 2012.

Glossary of Terms

(You will find these terms underlined or italicized throughout this text.)

abstract language   This language does not create an image. It is not concrete. Most nouns that end in -ism, -ion, -ness, or -ity are abstract. These words need definition because they are subjective.

ad hominem   A fallacy, a character attack that is irrelevant to the issue.

analogy   An extended comparison used to make the audience familiar with an abstract idea. It is like an extended, more complicated simile.

assertion   A claim put forward to make a case.

authority   Someone who has the education and experience to provide testimonial evidence to support a position.

assumption   Some knowledge based on education or experience that should be taken as a given. You can stipulate an assumption this way: "If we assume that most teenagers in most countries are not allowed to buy guns, then . . ."

bandwagoning   You go along with the crowd for no better reason than to fit in, conform. There should be another reason to "join." If there isn't, it's *bandwagoning*.

begging the question   Can be a statement, a question, or an answer. The question being begged is that posed by the person's explanation or question. The person speaking *assumes some fact not in evidence*.

3 Kinds of:
circular reasoning   Sometimes there is seeming evasion, where the listener is led around in circles. This particular kind of question begging is called *circular reasoning*. Here especially the question asked is just "begging" to be asked again. This is the most commonly accepted definition of begging the question in academic circles. Two other types are accepted in common use, by media, politicians, and lay people involved in analyzing arguments.

epithet   Another kind of question begging occurs when someone avoids an answer to the problem by labeling someone or something.

loaded question   A leading question, also called a *loaded question*. Here there is a stated question, there is an assumption made, and the question assumes a fact not in evidence.

causal premise   This kind of premise asserts some cause-effect connection. It usually contains a word such as "because" or "since." It is not an acceptable premise if it asserts only one cause or asserts an absolute. For example, "The reason kids shoot other kids in school is they are neglected at home" is not acceptable. "Since television has come on the scene, some people have stopped reading as many books as they used to before its advent" is more acceptable.

concession   A concession is when you concede, give up a point. For example, you might say, "Mr. X has a point. There is no real way to be sure Santa Claus does not exist."

concrete language   Concrete language is language that we can see or hear. It contains words that we can readily imagine. Sight words are a bit more objective than auditory ones.

contributing factor   These are events or situations that have contributed to the ultimate effect. Some pieces are more key than others. Some pieces are more concrete, or more necessary for us to have in order to connect the others. Contributing factors are just those that should be considered as possibly or probably adding to the outcome.

counterargument   The counterargument is the opponent's view. You should openly acknowledge and analyze it.

credibility   Credibility means believability. You should add relevant details, names and occupations and experiences of authorities or witnesses to add credibility.

deductive reasoning   This is reasoning from a general premise to a specific conclusion. When you organize an essay deductively, you begin with your thesis, or conclusion, and then present the supports.

definition premise   This is a premise that provides a clear definition of any abstract terms. It can also work like this: x is y. For example, if my premise is, "Mr. B is a womanizer," I am using a definition premise. In this case, the premise would be unacceptable because it is ad hominem and/or poisoning the well.

equivocation (equi+voce)   This means to give equal voice or value to a word or phrase even though it means different things in different contexts. If I am commenting on Mr. Bush's speech to a battered women's organization, and I say, "Mr. Bush says he is against violence, yet he advocates going to war against Iraq!" I am equivocating. The violence we see in domestic disputes is not the same as the violence of war.

ethos appeal   Appeal to author's goodness, reputation.

evidence Evidence is used to support your claims or premises. Physical items, witness testimony, studies, statistics, personal experiences (examples or illustrations), and historical facts can be considered evidence. Important note: Evidence must be qualified.

fact A fact is something that is considered true or certain since it can be objectively proven.

fallacy From *fallere* in Latin, which means "to deceive." A fallacy is misleading, leads away from understanding, away from truth. It may be committed either intentionally, as when a politician claims his opponent is an "ugly American," or unintentionally, due just to lack of reasoning or thoughtfulness. It may come in the form of an assertion, some sort of declaration or statement; it may be imbedded in a question, known as an interrogative; it may come in the form of a command, known as an imperative; or in the form of an exclamation of emotion. Fallacies are persuasive, so they are not very obvious mistakes in logic. The statement "pigs can fly" is not a fallacious statement, because it is absurd.

false analogy A false analogy occurs for two main reasons, either of which is sufficient to deem an analogy false: 1) There are too many dissimilar characteristics or 2) the two situations or conditions being compared are too incomparable, i.e., carry different weight. You should not compare being raped while wearing a short skirt to having your house burglarized since you left your front door open. You should also consider all of the elements present in two situations before making an analogy to make sure there are enough similarities.

false dilemma (either/or fallacy) Here one is given only a certain number of choices when indeed there are more: "You either love America or leave it." Notice the word "or," which is the usual signal or cue word for a possible false dilemma.

hidden assumption Some fact or value that one holds that is assumed but not stated. If I say, "Girls shouldn't go to war. War requires endurance and tolerance for violence," there is a hidden assumption that girls have less endurance and less tolerance for violence. There is also an assumption that war requires both. The second would be a safe assumption, while the first would probably cause an argument.

hyperbole (exaggeration) A hyperbolic statement is not qualified, and usually constitutes an absolute. There are cases where the words "all" or "always" can be legitimately used, such as in the sentences "All men are mortal" and "Living people always breathe." It's only a hyperbole, a statement that oversimplifies a case while exaggerating it, when the statement is clearly untrue: "Why do you always drink all of the milk?" your roommate might ask. You should use *qualifiers* to avoid hyperbole, which lessens your *credibility*.

hypothesis   A hypothesis can be used in many ways. It can be used as a premise in deductive argument (if x happens, y will follow). It can be used, as it usually is, in scientific studies that require inductive logic that seeks to prove a probability. It can also be used at the end of an argument essay to stimulate the reader's imagination, getting him/her to imagine possible or probable outcomes should something that has been proposed actually be implemented.

inductive reasoning   This is reasoning from specific to general. It is the kind of reasoning, from possibilities to probabilities, that scientists and criminologists use. The outcome of purely inductive research will not glean a definite answer, but rather at best put forward a probability after one has presented all of one's evidence.

inference   This is a conclusion drawn from evidence. One draws an inference once one has read or observed some phenomenon. The inference can be either logical or illogical.

Logos appeal   Appeal to one's sense of logic, evident especially when one uses words such as "consequently" or "therefore."

major premise   This is the most general, basic premise upon which you base your argument, and your syllogism, if you are constructing one. Major premises are noted for their lack of specific language. (All men are mortal.)

metaphor   A kind of figurative language that compares one thing to something else that is concrete. For a metaphor to be effective, the image should be quite concrete, familiar to one's audience and yet not overused. It differs from a simile in that there is a direct connection made between the two things being compared, no words such as "like" or "as" in between. If you like, you can think of there being an equal (=) sign between the two things: "Tom is a bear in the morning." (Tom = bear.) A metaphor should also be fitting, appropriate for the given context. We don't want to call Tom a bear if Tom is really a hairless little guy, unless our purpose is to create a sense of irony, of course.

minor premise   This is the more specific assertion that follows from the general, major premise. In categorical syllogisms, it is known as the *particular proposition*.

necessary conditions   A necessary condition refers to the result that must come about if the sufficient conditions are in place. Used to analyze causal arguments.

objective language Language that is factual, not subjective, is objective. Concrete words, numbers, dates, times, names, and places are objective. Objective language adds *credibility* to your assertions. Objective language is not slanted or biased.

omitting When a person omits, either intentionally or not, one leaves out pertinent information. Omitting such information is one way to slant a story and bias an audience.

oversimplification Although some authors of critical thinking texts see oversimplification as a separate fallacy, I have used it here to denote the basis of fallacious reasoning and even hyperbolizing. One leaves out considerations of relevant data and reduces a complex situation to its simplest explanation while creating a post hoc fallacy, for example.

pathos appeal Appeal to emotion; the guilt by association and other appeals on the fallacy list are such appeals. Pathos appeals are not necessarily fallacious, though.

personification When we personify something inhuman, we give it human characteristics. If I say, "The brow of America is furrowed over the latest election results," I am personifying America.

possibility In inductive logic, this is where we start. Possibilities are included and then excluded to get to a probability.

post hoc *Post hoc, ergo propter hoc* literally, denotatively means "after this, therefore because of this." When you link an effect to a cause *just* because the effect happened, in time, after some event, then you have post hoc, perhaps. B occurred after A; therefore A caused B.

premise A basic, general assertion of fact or value upon which you base your argument. An argument may have several premises.

probability What you get after you eliminate certain possibilities. In inductive logic, arriving at a probable outcome, cause, or reason is your goal.

qualifiers Relative qualifiers can add credibility and objectivity to your claims. Such words are "some," "usually," or "most." Use these words to avoid hyperbole.

question at issue This is the particular aspect of an issue on which you will for the moment, in your paragraph or in your discourse, concentrate.

refutation This is the rebuttal to the counterargument. You prove that the opponent's logic or evidence is flawed.

signal words   These are words used to show a quote or paraphrase from someone else's material. Example: "The author claims that . . ." or "According to Dr. Freud . . ."

simile   Similes are not the same as metaphors but they do compare two things that are seemingly different but share some aspect, as do metaphors. Unlike metaphors, similes use a comparative term in between the two things being compared. For example, I don't say that my husband *is* a beast in the morning, but rather say he acts *like* a beast. Comparative words such as "like," "than," or "as" signal a simile, as in "deader than a doornail."

slanting   Slanting occurs when authors or speakers use connotative language or omit certain relevant aspects of a circumstance or event. This method of presentation usually biases the audience. It is freely used and perhaps required by journalists writing pieces that qualify as "yellow journalism," the kind of journalism practiced in tabloids such as *The Inquirer*. Serious journalists, such as Walter Cronkite, considered such slanting unethical, and critical thinkers should avoid it. Ad hominem, epithet, and poisoning the well fallacies are cases of slanting.

slippery slope   Slippery slope fallacy occurs when people make predictions about future events that in all probability will not occur. The formula is "If x happens, y will occur." One way to tell you might have a slippery slope fallacy before you is if you see/hear the word "will." Example: "If Bert Cates is allowed to keep teaching in our public schools, our land will become like Sodom and Gomorrah, a land of pestilence and plague."

subjective language   Words that are subjective carry connotations and are more on the side of opinion than fact.

syllogism   Contains a major premise, a minor premise, and a conclusion. Part of deductive logic.

thesis   Usually comes at the end of the first paragraph in an argument essay. It is not a premise, but rather the conclusion you have reached after all of your research and writing. It contains an opinion and states your position. Does not have to be a pro or con position. May include limiting words like "might" or "perhaps."

tu quo que (you also fallacy)   A fallacy that occurs when someone claims the right to behave a certain way just because "you also" have done so. Example: "Why shouldn't I smoke? You do!"